T0320304

ROUTLEDGE LIBRARY EDITIONS: THE OIL INDUSTRY

Volume 1

THE BRITISH ECONOMY AFTER OIL

THE BRITISH ECONOMY
AFTER OIL

Manufacturing or Services?

Edited by
TERRY BARKER AND PAUL DUNNE

Routledge
Taylor & Francis Group
LONDON AND NEW YORK

First published in 1988 by Croom Helm

This edition first published in 2024
by Routledge
4 Park Square, Milton Park, Abingdon, Oxon OX14 4RN

and by Routledge
605 Third Avenue, New York, NY 10158

Routledge is an imprint of the Taylor & Francis Group, an informa business

British Library Cataloguing in Publication Data
A catalogue record for this book is available from the British Library

ISBN: 978-1-032-55944-5 (Set)
ISBN: 978-1-032-57573-5 (Volume 1) (hbk)
ISBN: 978-1-032-57574-2 (Volume 1) (pbk)
ISBN: 978-1-003-43993-6 (Volume 1) (ebk)

DOI: 10.4324/9781003439936

Publisher's Note
The publisher has gone to great lengths to ensure the quality of this reprint but points out that some imperfections in the original copies may be apparent.

Disclaimer
The publisher has made every effort to trace copyright holders and would welcome correspondence from those they have been unable to trace.

THE BRITISH ECONOMY AFTER OIL:

Manufacturing or Services?

Edited by

TERRY BARKER and PAUL DUNNE

CROOM HELM
London • New York • Sydney

Croom Helm Ltd, Provident House, Burrell Row,
Beckenham, Kent, BR3 1AT
Croom Helm Australia, 44-50 Waterloo Road,
North Ryde, 2113, New South Wales

Published in the USA by
Croom Helm
in association with Methuen, Inc.
29 West 35th Street
New York, NY 10001

British Library Cataloguing in Publication Data

The British economy after oil: manufacturing
    or services?
    1. Great Britain — Industries
    I. Barker, Terry II. Dunne, Paul
    338′.0941   HC256.6
    ISBN 0-7099-5064-0

Library of Congress Cataloging-in-Publication Data

The British economy after oil : manufacturing or services? / edited by
Terry Barker and Paul Dunne.
        p.   cm.
    Bibliography: p.
    ISBN 0-7099-5064-0
    1. Great Britain — Industries. 2. Economic forecasting — Great
Britain. 3. Great Britain — Economic conditions — 1945–   . 4. Great
Britain — Economic policy — 1945–   . 5. Great Britain —
Manufactures. 6. Service industries — Great Britain. I. Barker, Terry.
II. Dunne, Paul.
HC256.6.B76234   1988
338.0941 — dc 19
                                                              87-27555
                                                              CIP

Printed and bound in Great Britain by Mackays of Chatham Ltd, Kent

CONTENTS

TABLES

FIGURES

CONTRIBUTORS

John Barber	Senior Economic Advisor, Department of Trade and Industry, London
Terry Barker	Senior Research Officer, Department of Applied Economics, University of Cambridge
Ciaran Driver	Senior Lecturer, Thames Polytechnic, London
Paul Dunne	Research Officer, Department of Applied Economics, University of Cambridge and Fellow of Magdalene College, Cambridge
Wynne Godley	Director, Department of Applied Economics, University of Cambridge and Fellow of King's College, Cambridge
Andrew Kilpatrick	Economist, National Economic Development Office, Millbank, London
Christopher Moir	Economist, National Economic Development Office, Millbank, London
John Whitley	Principal Research Fellow, ESRC Macroeconomic Modelling Bureau, University of Warwick
David Williams	Economist, The Midland Bank, Group Economics Department, Head Office, London

FOREWORD

I am pleased to have been invited to contribute a Foreword to this important study on the British Economy After Oil. It takes as its starting point the report of the Select Committee of the House of Lords on Overseas Trade which met under the distinguished chairmanship of Lord Aldington. I was a member of that Select Committee. Indeed it was set up as a result of a debate I initiated in November 1983 when Britain started moving into an adverse balance on its trade in manufactured goods for the first time since the Industrial Revolution. That adverse balance has since widened.

The House of Lords Report, which was published in 1985, was primarily concerned with this trade deficit; but inevitably it dealt with wider aspects of Britain's industrial economy. It drew attention to the risk being run due to the progressive diminution in manufacturing, and the impact this could have, to the detriment of the economy as a whole, when the exceptional earnings from oil diminished.

This is the theme taken up and analysed in this book. It raises a fundamental issue about the future of our economy as we move into the next century. I hope it stimulates much more discussion.

Derek Ezra   House of Lords

PREFACE

This book has developed out of the debate following the House of Lords Report on Overseas Trade of 1985. The Cambridge Growth Project and Cambridge Econometrics held a joint conference on the subject in 1986: several of the conference papers have been updated and revised for publication in this book and several further chapters have been contributed by participants at the conference who did not give formal presentations.

We should like to thank the organisers and participants at the conference and all those who have commented on the papers and the draft book.

Since the conference, a considerable effort has gone into preparation of the book in the Department of Applied Economics, University of Cambridge. In particular we should like to thank Ann Newton, the Department's Publications Officer, for substantial editorial assistance, and Shirley Seal, who prepared the text for the laser printer. They have worked with patience and skill in coping with the many problems involved.

Finally, we should like to acknowledge the financial support of the Economic and Social Research Council and Cambridge Econometrics (1985) Ltd for the research work of the Cambridge Growth Project.

Terry Barker   Cambridge
Paul Dunne

INTRODUCTION

Terry Barker and Paul Dunne

Most commentators on the future of the UK economy are concerned about what will happen as North Sea oil runs out. The collapse of manufacturing in 1980-81 and its slow recovery thereafter has led to worries about how the economy will cope with the future loss of the oil windfall gains. Although some consider that there is no problem, arguing that there are strong favourable trends in the economy and that the future lies in the promotion and growth of services, others argue that the economic success of the UK requires the development of a strong manufacturing base so that manufacturing is in a position to take over from oil as a foreign exchange earner in the 1990s.

The Report of the House of Lords Select Committee on Overseas Trade in 1985 threw into relief these differing views over the structural weakness of the UK economy. The authors of the Report saw the move towards a dependence on manufactured imports, hidden in the overall balance of payments by the oil surplus, to be a worrying harbinger of economic stagnation. The UK Chancellor of the Exchequer, on the other hand, could not see that there was any problem at all.

It is against this background that in June 1986 a joint conference was held by the Cambridge Growth Project and Cambridge Econometrics on manufacturing and services. The revised contributions from that conference, together with several papers solicited to give a more comprehensive coverage of the debate, provide the material for this book.

All of the contributions represent the views of their respective authors and so there is no collective position on any of the issues. This proves, in fact, to be a strength of the book, since it provides insight into the kind of disagreements which are found in the policy debate.

In Chapter 1 Professor Wynne Godley, Director of the Department of Applied Economics at Cambridge and leader of the Cambridge Economic Policy Group (CEPG), assesses the future of manufacturing and the UK economy. The CEPG provided the gloomy predictions of economic decline and mass unemployment in the 1970s that some commentators and politicians brushed aside, or attacked, but which turned out to be surprisingly accurate. His assessment of the Thatcher experiment makes sobering reading and provides an introduction to the manufacturing vs services debate firmly on the side of manufacturing.

Godley criticises the debate of economic policy as pre-occupied with the short run when the real issues are fundamental trends which require a longer-run perspective. He attacks the critics of the House of Lords Committee for complacency in the face of strong evidence of structural problems. The relative failure of the UK in manufacturing, the scale of the replacement of trade in manufactures by trade in oil and services as import penetration increases, and the intractability of the unemployment problem given the continuation of present trends, all contribute to a gloomy picture of future prospects.

Chapter 2, by Terry Barker, Head of the Cambridge Growth Project (CGP), presents another Cambridge view, using the CGP model of the UK economy. This is an interindustry dynamic model which combines macroeconomic relations determining the exchange rate, average earnings and consumers' expenditures with a model of industrial structure. This makes it the most disaggregated of the UK macromodels and the only one which can analyse structural change at an industrial level. He considers the industrial structure and future prospects of international trade, and comes to a similar conclusion to that of Chapter 1.

Barker contrasts the House of Lords Committee view and the Treasury view, looking at the characterisics of the oil, manufacturing and services sectors and the changing structure of UK trade. This shows that manufacturing has taken the whole burden of adjustment to the oil and gas increases and that as the oil is depleted through the 1990s both services and manufacturing are needed to close the prospective energy gap in the balance of payments. The prospects for the UK to the year 2000 are then considered, summarising the 1987 post-Budget Cambridge Econometrics forecast. The CGP model is then used to simulate the effects of two possible future policies to cure the balance of payments deficits, namely exchange-rate depreciation and an effective incomes policy, and to analyse how they might effect manufacturing and services. In both cases manufacturing increases as a share of output but its contribution to the balance of payments is negative for depreciation and positive for incomes policy. The House of Lords Committee's recommendations are considered in the light of this evidence.

In Chapter 3 John Whitley, of the ESRC Macroeconomic Modelling Bureau at the University of Warwick, considers the different approaches to disaggregation in the major UK models. The models now have the decline in manufacturing base as part of their sample experience, so any possible bias against services in favour of manufacturing in the simulation properties of the model can be investigated. The methods of disaggregation in the models are compared and the results of a common set of macroeconomic shocks to the models are reported. The responses differ markedly betweeen models and shocks. Only the CGP model used in the previous chapter is found to provide an adequate framework for the analysis of structural change.

John Barber, a senior economist at the Department of Trade and Industry, though writing in his own capacity, provides an international dimension to the debate by comparing experience in different countries in Chapter 4. He analyses the decline in the share of manufacturing since the 1960s in the UK in the context of what was happening in other countries, arguing that the shift from manufactures is not new and not peculiar to the UK and that there are a number of reasons for it which are common to all OECD countries.

In Chapter 5 Ciaran Driver from Thames Polytechnic, who wrote his contribution while working at NEDO, investigates the linkages between the service industries and other sectors, particularly manufacturing. Using input-output data, he investigates the effects on employment income of autonomous changes in industry output. This provides useful information on the interrelations and level of interdependence of the different industries, which illustrates the relation between service and manufactures and leads to a number of interesting conclusions.

In Chapter 6, Paul Dunne of the CGP looks at the structure and future prospects of service employment in the UK. The analysis is at two levels: he looks both at long-term trends by comparing sectoral employment and services industry employment over a long period of time, and at more detailed information on recent developments in the dynamic service industries. He finds great structural change taking place in industries, making the assessment of future prospects for employment difficult. Furthermore, some of the greatest recent growth is in sectors of service industry we know little about.

The main conclusions are that the service sector is unlikely to provide a cure for unemployment unless there is strong growth in domestic manufacturing, and that future growth in service employment will show rapidly changing skill demand, with continued demand for female part-time workers, and possibly increasing casualisation. The flexibility required of the labour market implies the need for high levels of investment in social infrastructure.

David Williams, an economist at the Midland Bank writing in his own capacity, provides in Chapter 7 an analysis of changes in the structure of manufacturing industry and its relation to banking and the changes in the financial markets. He illustrates the growing complexity of the relationship between corporate customers and commercial banks, with financial innovation increasing pressures and competition. This has led to a greater role for the industrial economist.

Finally, Chapter 8 by Andrew Kilpatrick and Christopher Moir, of the National Economic Development Office, considers developments in the UK's international trading performance. Kilpatrick and Moir find, as did Barker in Chapter 2, that the oil surplus has shifted the burden of adjustment on to the manufacturing sector. There have been some benefits from the restructuring in the form of higher productivity but the earnings from service exports are not large enough to bear the burden of adjustment of the adverse trends in manufacturing trade. Their analysis suggests that manufacturing must improve and that it might well be starting to do so. But a major improvemment in non-price competitiveness is required in manufacturing, and a policy is needed to sustain the growth of trade in services. Unfortunately, the established problems in consumer goods industries are now beginning to emerge in capital goods industries, with damaging implications for any future attempt to increase growth. It is important to give priority to the capital goods sector so that any expansion does not just draw in capital goods imports. This is relevant to both manufactures and services.

In any attempt to deal with the fundamental problems facing the UK economy no collection of this nature will provide complete coverage. However, the contributions to this volume address particularly important policy issues and present various aspects and positions in the debate.

The UK has undergone major and painful structural adjustments following the increase in production in North Sea oil. This came at the same time, 1980-81, as a new government was introducing radical monetarist policies, and indeed partly enabled the government to carry out these policies. Fortunately, the period of adjustment to the decline in oil production is likely to be much lengthier, giving more opportunity for the encouragement of replacement exports. Nevertheless, it is clear from the analyses in this book that there are important and difficult policy decisions to be faced.

If there is any consensus in the contributions to this book, it is that there needs to be some policy to strengthen manufacturing as the sector which is likely to play a major part in the post-oil economy. The reliance on a future 'service economy' to provide the required growth of export earnings in the 1990s is placing too much faith on the continued stability and growth of international financial markets with all their history of periodic speculation and collapse.

MANUFACTURING AND THE FUTURE
OF THE BRITISH ECONOMY

Wynne Godley

1.1 The Thatcher experiment

Since 1979 the British economy has been the subject of an experiment which successive Conservative governments have been trying to represent as having been a success. My view is that the experiment has already demonstrably failed and that, unless it is abandoned and a proper strategy now adopted, things will get much worse within the next few years.

It was in the mid seventies that there was a remarkable change in the political mood of the country. Until then there had been overwhelming support for the idea that governments could and therefore should maintain full employment. From then on it has been generally held that governments cannot maintain full employment and, therefore, should not try. As recently as 1973 expansionary measures taken by Mr Heath, with the overwhelming support of public opinion, brought unemployment down to about half a million. Yet within a year or two, this consensus had utterly fallen apart. After twenty-five years of full employment, previously attributed to the way governments had run the economy, the view quite suddenly came to be held that, if governments tried to maintain full employment by traditional means, they would fail to do so and only generate inflation.

It is important to recall that the crucial change of opinion did not occur when Mrs Thatcher came to power. It happened well before that, under a Labour government. I date it from Mr Healey's famous return from Heathrow in subjugation to the directives of the IMF and the disinflation which he subsequently undertook. In any event, it was under a Labour government that unemployment first really took off, rising to one and a quarter million in 1976 and hovering there until 1979.

The view that governments would be wrong to try and influence unemployment was, of course, greatly reinforced and elaborated by Mrs Thatcher. Indeed, she sponsored a comprehensive redefinition of the role of government in relation to economic policy. The proper course of action, the story now went, was to set stringent targets for public borrowing and for the money supply which were to extend several years into the future. But new incentives would be given through the tax system and in other ways, which would somehow release the energies of sleepy British people. This would be the way to regenerate the economy. The response would be a large, rapid and permanent improvement in inflation. The cost might be a small rise in unemployment but, it was argued, this would only be temporary.

Although the government did not regard it as within its power directly to influence unemployment, it did believe that its policies, if firmly adhered to, would in the end *lead* to full employment. It was largely on unemployment, after all, that the Conservatives fought and won the 1979 election.

The outcome was rather different. As everyone knows, unemployment has risen to between three and four million and no one seems to think that much of a fall is now in prospect. Huge disparities have opened up within Britain, with miserable conditions of life in parts of Scotland, in the North, in Ireland, in Wales, in the West Midlands and of course in the inner cities. Recently thriving industrial areas have been going into a state of decay which begins to look chronic. The government seems proud of its record on production yet the average growth rate since it came to power has been well under half the *average* rate of growth between 1950 and 1974.

The money supply has not been under control at all. Seemingly as a result of the deregulation of financial institutions, there has been an explosion of net lending to the personal sector, with total indebtedness doubling, from £85 billion to £191 billion, between 1981 and 1985. It was this expansion of lending which gave rise to the huge increase in sterling M3 (control of which was supposed to be essential if inflation was to be brought down) and to even larger increases in the broader measures of liquid assets.

There has been very little improvement in domestic inflation. To begin with (between 1979 and 1981) cost inflation actually accelerated, partly as a response to the large increase in VAT in the 1979 budget. Inflation of domestic costs fell back in the early eighties but has recently been rising again; it is now very similar to that inherited by the first Thatcher government and considerably higher than that experienced by almost all Britain's competitors.

The recent fall in price inflation, for which the government takes much credit, is of course mainly the result of the fall (20 per cent since the beginning of 1985) in the price of oil and imported raw materials. Unless wage inflation is drastically moderated - and at present there is no sign of this - the medium-term expectation must be that price inflation will accelerate again.

In sum, for whatever reason, the consequence of government policy has so far been the opposite of what was intended. The rise in unemployment has been rapid, large and apparently permanent. The reduction in inflation has been precarious, long-drawn-out and imperfect.

1.2 Prospects for the future

The public discussion of economic prospects concentrates to an excessive degree on the very short term - a year or two at most. But it is to a much more distant time horizon that we should be looking. And it is the medium-term future which looks pretty grim. For some years leading industrialists have expressed views about the medium-term future of the British economy, and indeed Britain itself, which are surprisingly vehement and even apocalyptic. For instance, a House of Lords Select Committee on Overseas Trade concluded in 1985 that present policies and events 'constitute a grave threat to the standard of living and to the economic and political stability of the nation'. More recently Sir Edwin Nixon, the head of IBM in Britain, went so far as to say that unless things change 'we had better get used to continuing decline - and in its wake social and political decay and perhaps even democracy itself struggling for survival'.

These warnings were not concerned with the social and political implications of our having at present over three million unemployed. What they were saying is that we have a new strategic problem of alarming proportions. It will manifest itself in a depression worse and far more divisive even than the one we have now, unless strategic policy decisions are taken soon.

The Lords' Select Committee Report was rudely and hastily dismissed by the Chancellor of the Exchequer, and it was rubbished or lampooned by financial journalists close to the government.

Is it the case that a new kind of economic strategy is urgently needed? Is it true, as the Lords' Select Committee put it, that 'Failure to recognise [the] dangers now could have a devastating effect on the future of the nation . . . the situation in which we find ourselves is not self-correcting: things will not come right of their own accord. Urgent action is required not only by government but by everyone'. Or is it the case, as the government would have it, that the whole thing is just a piece of special pleading for congenial feather-bedding which should be ignored.

I think that the issue does indeed mainly turn, as the Lords' Committee maintained, on the future performance of our manufacturing industry; and that the future of British manufacturing is in serious jeopardy.

Consider first what may be called the 'complacent' view, which is to be found in the evidence given by the Chancellor and the Treasury to the Lords' Committee.

First (they say), while there has indeed been a decline in manufacturing industry, this is not a specifically British problem. Everywhere in the world the employment and income generated by manufacturing industry have been falling as shares of total employment and total income. Second, this falling proportion is a consequence of the fact that as countries grow richer they want to buy services more than manufactured goods. Third, our balance of trade in manufactured goods has certainly deteriorated in the last ten years. But this deterioration had to happen because of a rising surplus in our trade in oil. The balance of payments, after all, has to balance. Fourth, the prospective fall in oil production is not a serious cause for concern. Just as the rise in oil production caused the balance of trade in manufactures to fall, the fall in oil production will somehow restore the favourable balance in manufactures.

The government argues that two further factors will see us through the period of declining oil production. The balance of trade in services should continue to improve, and we should be earning a rising income on our assets overseas, the net value of which has greatly increased.

These are the arguments for feeling happy and doing nothing. I think it is quite easy to show that, taken together, they are wrong.

It is true that manufacturing employment and income have fallen as shares of total employment and income in most industrial countries. However, the meaning of this is very ambiguous. A fall in manufacturing employment may happen because productivity has risen particularly fast; in the extreme case, productivity may have risen so much that the whole of manufacturing output could be produced by a single man sitting at a computer terminal which operated robots throughout the country. The proportion of people employed in manufacturing would have fallen to virtually nil, but the productivity of that single man - the quantity of manufactured goods he produced - would be stupendous: he would be able to run even the Japanese out of business and supply the entire world with manufactures. The country would be extremely prosperous because the proceeds from the sale of manufactured goods could be used to buy imports of materials and employ the rest of the population in producing services and other goods.

On the other hand, a fall in employment in manufacturing may be the result of such *slow* growth in productivity that industry is not competitive and its output cannot all be sold.

Unfortunately Britain is in the second category. Indeed, if we measure quantities of goods produced, we find that *Britain is the only advanced industrial economy* in which manufacturing output has increased less than the output of other goods and services. Taking the period since 1960, the relative decline in manufacturing output is a uniquely British phenomenon. And this relative decline in manufacturing output, to come to the second point, did not happen because British consumers decided to spend less on manufactured goods. Indeed, in the recent period of so-called recovery since 1981, spending on manufactures has risen about twice as fast as other kinds of spending.

Figure 1.1   *Growth of GDP and manufacturing output*

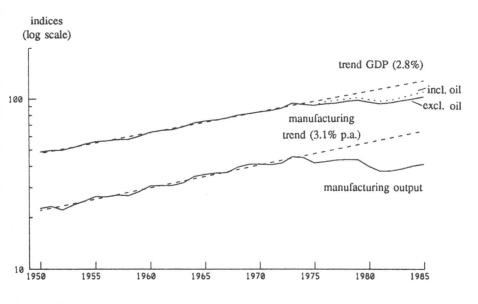

Source: *Economic Trends.*

The reason for the decline of British manufacturing output has nothing to do with any preference for services; it is simply that a rapidly rising proportion of our supplies has come from abroad while foreign demand for our exports has not risen commensurately. The magnitudes are remarkable. For instance, as shown in Fig. 1.1, manufacturing output is now 10 per cent lower absolutely than it was in 1973. Yet imports of manufactures have *more than doubled* over the same period. Or take the period of so-called recovery during the last four years. Output has risen about 10 per cent since the trough in 1981 but imports of manufactures have risen more than 44 per cent over the same period.

Figure 1.2   *Balance of trade in manufacturing (1985 export prices)*

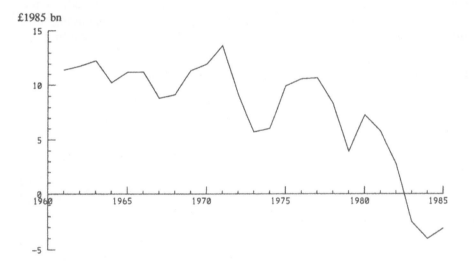

Source: UK CSO *Pink Book*, 1985, HMSO.

As Fig. 1.2 illustrates, there was a large surplus which was roughly constant at eight or nine billion pounds (measured at 1980 prices) between 1960 and 1977. But to see what was really going on it is necessary to look at exports separately from imports. If we do this we find that imports rose by over 300 per cent, while exports rose by only 140 per cent. The fact that the absolute gap between exports and imports at the beginning of the period was much the same as at the end, completely obscures the fact that imports rose about twice as fast as exports. And as Fig. 1.3 suggests, import penetration has continued to increase rapidly since 1977, while the share of UK exports of manufactures in world trade fell in 1985 to an all-time low.

Figure 1.3 *Exports and imports of manufactures as a percentage of domestic spending on manufactures*

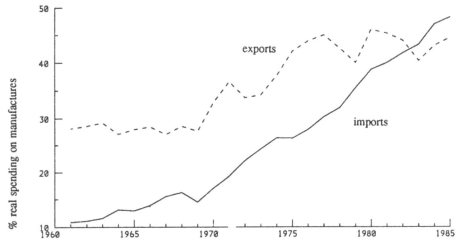

Source: Authors' estimates.

I think that the strategic problem was correctly identified by the Lords' Select Committee and that it is indeed extremely serious. To assess the dimensions of the problem, it is essential to extend the time horizon well beyond the one- or two-year outlook normally covered by forecasters. The processes which are of such concern work quite slowly and it is possible, with good fortune, that no serious deterioration will occur for a year or two. It is only by focusing attention on prospective developments over the next decade or so that we can properly identify the magnitude of the underlying difficulties which now confront us.

The intractability of the unemployment problem is illustrated in Fig. 1.4. The change in unemployment is plotted against the annual average change in output over every five-year period from 1950-55 until 1980-85. One striking feature of these figures is that there has not been a single five-year period since the war when there was any significant fall in unemployment. They also show that unemployment rose over every five-year period in which the rise in output was less than 2.5 per cent

Figure 1.4   *Changes in output and employment over 5-year overlapping periods, 1950-1985*

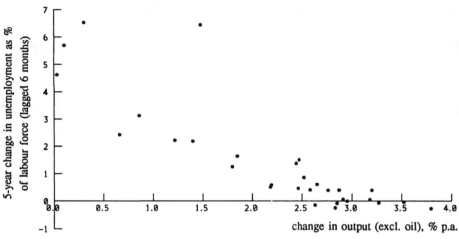

Source: *Economic Trends.*

p.a.[1] and also that growth rates of up to 3-3.5 per cent p.a. have generally been required to ensure that unemployment does not increase. The chart suggests that to get unemployment down by as little as 1 per cent (250,000) over the next five years output would have to grow by at least 3.5 per cent a year and probably more.

The scale and nature of the strategic problem may be encapsulated in the following propositions.

(1) The minimum rate of growth of total real income and output necessary to keep unemployment constant at 3-4 million is probably 2.5 per cent p.a.

(2) On past form the growth in domestic demand for manufactures will be at least as fast as that of total real national income.

(3) Continuation of anything like past trends of trade in manufactures - exports as a share of world trade and imports as a share of domestic

---

1   For this reason I cannot agree with the projection in *NIESR* (1986). This suggested that unemployment will remain constant over the next five years with non-oil output growing at only 1.6 per cent p.a. Past experience suggests that such slow growth would be associated with a rise of 1 or 2 per cent p.a. (250-500,000) in unemployment.
    It is possible that demographic factors will in future make it a little easier to get unemployment down, particularly after 1990. According to official estimates (Department of Employment, 1985), the labour force (assuming constant unemployment) will rise by about 750,000 between 1985 and 1990. Most of this increase arises from higher participation by women, which will probably slow down after 1990.

demand - implies that the deficit trade in manufactured goods will rise several fold over the next decade. According to my estimates, even if rather favourable assumptions are made about world trade and the rate of exchange, this deficit will rise from £3 billion in 1985 to nearly £25 billion (at 1985 prices) in the mid nineties. This estimate ignores the fact that net investment in manufacturing industry has been negative since 1979 and that manufacturing industry is probably already becoming constrained by shortages of capacity and skilled manpower.

(4) Soon after 1990, assuming a sustained growth rate of only 2 per cent p.a - the minimum necessary to prevent unemployment from rising - we shall become net importers of energy. The balance of trade in oil will therefore move from a surplus of £8 billion in 1985 to some negative number after 1990.

(5) It is extremely implausible that net exports of services and net income from abroad will spontaneously expand on a scale which can anywhere near make good the loss on oil and manufactures.

While the uncertainties about the ten-year prospects are very large indeed, the problems looked at *ex ante* seem so enormous as to give rise to extremely serious concern. It may be possible for a number of years to sustain the growth of output by borrowing abroad. Some other countries (for instance the US and Ireland) have managed to run deficits on the scale (when expressed as a proportion of their GDP) which we are now considering.

Such borrowing could not, however, be sustainable as a long-term strategy. The UK would quite quickly - within ten or fifteen years - become a net debtor nation and thus incur a rapidly growing burden of debt interest. To maintain total output by foreign borrowing would also imply that the underlying deterioration in manufacturing output and trading performance would be continuing, so that the position would be weaker than ever when borrowing became impossible. And the UK would also then be starting to import energy, probably at higher prices than now.

If, on the other hand, the government were to keep the current account in balance by deflation alone, then output could probably grow at only 1-1.5 per cent p.a. Growth as low as this has in the past been associated with a rise in unemployment at a rate of about 100,000 a year, so it might exceed 4 million by 1995 using present measurement conventions, or close to 5 million using pre-Thatcher methods. Further changes in classification or the extension of job-creation measures might of course prevent actual recorded figures reaching such a high level.

The only remaining conventional option is progressive devaluation. But again the trends seem so adverse that the real devaluation necessary to sustain the growth of exports relative to that of imports (given that output rises at a respectable rate) would have to be so large that the implications for inflation might be unacceptable.

2

INTERNATIONAL TRADE
AND THE BRITISH ECONOMY

Terry Barker

2.1 Introduction

The collapse of oil prices has brought forward the time when the balance of payments will once again emerge as a constraint on growth and higher employment in the British economy. There is no dispute about this between the various forecasters; a £1 bn deficit has emerged for 1986 and, although there has been a move back into surplus in 1987, all the major groups are expecting the balance of payments to move into deficit in 1988 with not much prospect (apart from that of a sudden and very substantial increase in oil prices) of any improvement. The situation will be a familiar one, since it was characteristic of the British economy before North Sea oil began to make a substantial contribution to the supply of foreign exchange.

This chapter explores the nature of this balance-of-payments constraint and the roles played by manufacturing and services in creating it. The exploration is done in the context of the post-budget forecast for the economy for the next 14 years, carried out by Cambridge Econometrics (CE) in April 1987 using the Cambridge Growth Project's Multisectoral Dynamic Model (MDM).

Section 2.2 of this chapter introduces the debate on manufactures and services in the context of the prospects for the British economy and examines the economic characteristics of the different sectors. Section 2.3 looks at developments in exports, imports and the balance of payments from 1954 through to the substantial production and net export of oil in the 1980s. The structural changes underlying these developments are analysed and the question is addressed of whether recent experience has led to any improvement. Section 2.4 goes on to examine the prospects for the balance of payments in terms of the contributions of oil, manufactures and services, drawing on the Cambridge Econometrics post-budget forecast.

Section 2.5 then takes two policies, exchange-rate depreciation and an effective incomes policy, each of which reduces the deficits, and discusses how they will affect manufactures and services. Finally, Section 2.6 turns to the controversy over whether manufactures in particular should be encouraged by policy measures, as advocated by the House of Lords Select Committee on Overseas Trade.

2.2 Manufacturing and structural weakness in the British economy

The debate

There is a yawning gap between those who see an emerging problem of crisis proportions and those who see little cause for concern. On the one hand Lord Aldington, commenting on the evidence of the dramatic lurch of the balance of trade in manufactures into deficit in 1982-84, says:

> . . . this Committee, on the evidence produced to it, considers that there is something fairly near a crisis for the country in the situation that has developed over the manufacturing industries' balance of trade (UK House of Lords, 1985, vol. II *Oral Evidence*).

On the other hand, the Chancellor and his Treasury advisors see the deficit as evidence of a shift in comparative advantage away from manufactures to services and other activities and a reflection of market forces which will solve, by themselves, any potential problem in due course:

> I am puzzled as to why you should think that, if it [the manufacturing sector] were to decline, not in absolute terms but as a share of GDP, that would be a cause for concern. I honestly do not understand that (UK House of Lords, 1985, *ibid.*)

These opposing views are set out in detail in the pages that follow.

CONCLUSIONS OF THE REPORT OF THE HOUSE OF LORDS SELECT COMMITTEE ON OVERSEAS TRADE

(1) The balance of trade in manufactures moved sharply into deficit in 1983. The threat posed by this development is being hidden by surpluses on the balance of trade in oil.

(2) It is a development that was brought about by poor export performance and high import penetration across a wide spectrum of manufacturing industry.

(3) The poor export performance was due to the long-term factors of low levels of investment and cost competitiveness and 'cultural' problems and to the short-term factor of the high sterling exchange rate of 1979-82.

(4) It would be prudent for the Government to plan on the basis that there may be no oil surpluses by 1990 and a return to deficit by the end of the century.

(5) Urgent action is needed to revive manufacturing, for the following reasons:

- service industry cannot substitute for manufacturing, because many services are dependent on manufacturing and only 20% of services are traded overseas

- there is no reason to expect any automatic resurgence of manufacturing: its decline was not inevitable, new industries require a long timescale for development and lost markets are difficult to regain.

(6) If action is not taken, the country will experience adverse effects including:

- a contraction of manufacturing to the point at which successful continuation in much of manufacturing activity is at risk

- an irreplaceable loss of GDP

- a balance of payments so adverse that severe deflation would be needed

- higher unemployment, and lower tax revenue for public spending

- stagnation of the economy, with rising inflation driven up by a falling exchange rate.

(See UK House of Lords, 1985, vol. I, p. 82)

THE TREASURY VIEW

There is concern in some quarters about what is going to happen as the output of North Sea oil declines, but we believe that just as there were adjustments as the oil came on stream, through the mechanism of the real exchange rate, so something very similar will happen as the output falls. The real exchange rate will decline and make other sectors more competitive. What sectors these will be, whether manufacturing or services, we are not in a position to say. The aim of policy is to put in place the framework which allows the most efficient and competitive activities to emerge at the time in question (UK House of Lords, 1985, vol. II, Q352).

We have seen more than just a reflection in manufacturing of the turnround in the oil account (1980-84). It is difficult to resist the conclusion that our comparative advantage in trading terms in manufacturing is rather less than it is in some other non-oil sectors of the economy, such as agriculture, other visible trade and services (ibid., Q281).

The concern about what will happen to the economy as the output of oil declines is exaggerated, for the following reasons:
- the surplus on trade in fuel will diminish only at a gradual pace
- the balance on non-fuel trade will tend to improve, responding in part to a fall in the real exchange rate
- it is possible that the trend by which services provide increasing surpluses to the balance of payments will continue (ibid., Q1618).

The debate is in the context of what will happen as the oil surplus on the balance of payments diminishes, either through the effect of the fall in oil prices 1985/86, or through the decline in North Sea oil production which is expected to take place gradually over the next 15 years or so. Clearly there is going to be a substantial fall in oil revenues, but this may simply mean that the balance of payments will move back out of chronic surplus (which has existed since 1980) into a balance in which exports and property income from the external reserves built up from the oil surplus will pay for the desired imports.

Structural weakness in the economy

The view taken in this chapter is that the cause for concern lies not so much in the manufacturing deficit as in the evidence that the basic features of the British economy brought out in the earlier debate on de-industrialisation (Blackaby (ed.), 1979) remain intact despite the changes in attitudes and legislation over the years since 1979. These features are best described as structural trends of the economy towards relatively low growth, high unemployment and high inflation, all in comparison with other industrialised Western economies.

Underlying these structural trends are the estimated values of income and price elasticities, responses of wage inflation to unemployment and investment to output, and other structural parameters which when taken together imply that the balance of payments will tend to restrict growth and keep it below that necessary for full employment. With a flexible exchange rate, the balance-of-payments constraint is translated into an inflation constraint because a balance-of-payments crisis is anticipated by the foreign exchange market in the form of a fall in sterling, causing a rise in import prices and hence in inflation more generally.

Two factors have obscured these relationships in recent years: first, the increase in North Sea oil production and consequent reduction in the foreign-exchange cost of oil has completely, but only temporarily, removed the balance-of-payments constraint; and second, the enormous expansion of the foreign exchange markets dating particularly from the first oil-price rises of 1973-74 has meant that exchange-rate movements are dominated by capital flows rather than current-account items on the balance of payments. Nevertheless, the short-term capital flows do respond to trends in the current account and it may be no coincidence that the exchange-rate crisis of spring 1985, when the sterling rate threatened to fall to $1 to £1, followed a period of current-account deficits, with the first quarter deficit of 1985 being the largest over the whole period from 1979 to spring 1986.

Although the debate is largely in terms of the weakness of manufacturing and the need, or otherwise, of special policies in favour of manufacturing, the problems are ones of unemployment and inflation. There is a structural weakness in the manufacturing sector in that imports of manufactures respond much more to a rise in domestic incomes than exports of manufactures respond to a rise in foreign incomes. However, this is partly compensated by a structural strength in the services sector. It may be just as easy or important to strengthen services even more as to improve the performance of manufacturing.

The economic characteristics of oil, manufactures and services

The House of Lords Report and much of the evidence given to the Committee implies that manufacturing, which contributes just over 20 per cent to GDP and 50 per cent to exports, is somehow better than other activities, particularly services. Since this issue is central to the topic of this book it is worth exploring further.

Different economic activities can be judged according to:
- the value the market (including government) puts on their output
- the employment they provide in location, including its quantity and quality (the last of these including healthy conditions, with opportunities for creativity and general satisfaction)
- the contribution they make to the balance of payments, helping to pay for imports of manufactures, food and basic materials
- their social costs in terms of actual or potential externalities such as pollution, congestion and degradation of the natural environment
- their potential for economic disruption (primary-product industries with international markets such as oil face severely fluctuating prices)
- their potential for economic growth via innovation and economies of scale.

These attributes cannot all simply be translated into present net market values because, first, the economy may not be at full employment; second, the balance of payments may become a severe constraint on policy; and third, there may be externalities.

The main economic characteristics of oil, manufacturing and services can be briefly summarised.

1) *Characteristics of the oil industry*:
- production is from an exhaustible natural resource and requires negligible amounts of labour
- the immediate economic effects of the industry are highly localised and the income flows are very concentrated
- oil is an almost perfectly tradeable commodity and its price has tended

to fluctuate dramatically.

These features make the oil and gas industry totally unsuitable as the basis of long-term growth in income and employment. The benefits of the industry are either temporary and localised or dependent on governments' using the tax revenues from oil to reduce other taxes, reduce borrowing or increase spending.

2) *Characteristics of manufacturing*:
- manufacturing generates more employment than oil but less than many services
- production usually has a high potential for economies of scale and technical change
- the industry is less localised than oil and its income flows are more diffused
- its output is tradeable but with substantial opportunities for product variety
- prices tend to be administered and much less volatile than prices of primary products.

The combination of tradeable output and economies of specialisation and scale have made particular manufacturing sectors either very successful in generating exports and economic growth (consumer electronic industries in Japan) or very vulnerable to foreign competition (the UK motor vehicle industry in the 1970s). Manufacturing industries provide a much firmer base for economic growth than oil, with a high potential for innovation, enormous export markets and strong backward and forward linkages with the rest of the economy.

However, in the particular circumstances of the British economy, with a large and relatively obsolete capital stock in manufacturing already, any expansion of manufacturing is likely to lead to further reductions in employment as old equipment is replaced by new machines operating with perhaps a fraction of the labour previously required.

3) *Characteristics of service industries*:
Services are much too heterogeneous to be considered as one economic activity. Their identifying characteristic is that they are transferred from seller to buyer as they are produced, i.e. they are not embodied in goods which can, even for a short time, be stocked. The most useful division for present purposes is that between
- personal services (hotels and catering, household services, recreation, entertainment)
- producer or intermediate services (finance, distribution, transport)
- social services (education and health)
- preventive services (defence, public administration, law and order).

If only the marketed services are considered (personal services and producer services) then their economic characteristics are as follows, although these remain considerable generalisations.

Personal services have:
- a high ratio of employment to output (combination of low wage rates and low capital cost)
- low economies of scale (although there are some, e.g. franchising in catering, hotel chains, mass spectator sports, TV entertainment)
- international trade restricted to tourist expenditures
- widely distributed markets across regions and occupational groups with very diffused income flows.

Producer services have:
- high ratio of employment to output
- a potential for substantial economies of scale (banking, insurance, transport, distribution)
- an income elasticity above one
- a tendency for value and volume shares to rise, partly through 'contracting out' of services previously classified as manufacturing
- widely distributed markets across regions and diffused income flows.

In addition some producer services (financial services, sea and air transport) are traded internationally, with services overall contributing a substantial and increasing net surplus to the balance of payments which reached £5.7 bn in 1985, falling slightly to £5.3 bn in 1986 (UK CSO, *Economic Trends*, April 1987).

The great advantage of the service industries in an economy faced with the prospect of high and rising unemployment is their high capacity for employment, but there is also the potential for large economies of scale and innovation in some services combined with opportunities to earn foreign exchange in increasing amounts.

2.3 Oil, manufactures and services and the UK balance of payments, 1954-85

This section is concerned mainly with the historical development of UK trade and the balance of payments. The emphasis is on the structural changes in exports and imports and the effects of oil on the economy.

The structure of trade

The structural change in foreign trade is dominated by the trend towards more openness of the economy and the increasing share of manufactures

Table 2.1   *The structure of UK overseas trade, 1954-81*

per cent

	1954	1973	1981
Exports			
food, drink & tobacco	7.3	4.7	5.9
basic materials	6.1	4.5	4.8
fuels	6.4	4.3	9.3
manufactures	55.3	55.1	53.0
services	24.8	31.3	27.1
total	100.0	100.0	100.0
Imports			
food, drink & tobacco	34.7	15.4	13.2
basic materials	13.3	9.0	8.9
fuels	14.8	18.4	7.8
manufactures	17.2	39.9	52.3
services	20.0	17.2	17.8
total	100.0	100.0	100.0

Notes: (1) These shares are based on values of exports and imports in constant prices.
(2) Manufacturing in this table and Tables 2.2 and 2.4 is defined on the SITC basis to exclude food, drink and tobacco manufactures. Elsewhere in the chapter manufacturing is on the SIC basis and includes food manufacturing.
Source: Barker (forthcoming).

in imports. Table 2.1 shows the shares of different types of commodities in exports and imports. The increasing share of manufactures in imports, from 17 per cent in 1954 to 52 per cent in 1981, stands out as the main change, but the fall in fuel imports as a result of North Sea oil, from 18 per cent in 1973 to 8 per cent in 1981, is also dramatic. The decline in service exports 1973-81 is primarily the result of a fall in export revenues from sea transport.

Export and import elasticities

Table 2.2 shows estimated elasticities and trends from the export and import functions incorporated into MDM, aggregated into 5 main groups. The most important structural feature in these estimates is the very high activity elasticity for imported manufactures, with a value of 2.8, implying that for a 10 per cent increase in domestic expenditures, manufactured imports will rise by 28 per cent *ceteris paribus*. In addition to this activity effect, a strong upward trend of 3.7 per cent p.a. is estimated, with the only compensation for this trend being a high

Table 2.2   *Activity and price elasticities for UK overseas trade*

	Activity elasticity	Price elasticity	Trend (%p.a.)
Exports			
food, drink & tobacco	0.88	-0.84	0.0
basic materials	0.48	-1.32	0.0
fuels	0.13	-0.49	0.0
manufactures	0.76	-0.90	0.1
services	1.07	-1.40	0.0
total	0.78	-1.01	0.1
Imports			
food, drink & tobacco	1.14	-0.14	-1.9
basic materials	0.41	-0.80	1.7
fuels	0.90	-0.62	-1.2
manufactures	2.80	-1.48	3.7
services	2.05	-0.02	-5.9
total	2.14	-0.96	0.9

Note: These elasticities and trends are aggregated from estimates for 40 export and import commodities. Within services, transport and communications trade is related to total visible trade as the activity variable, other commodity exports are related to industrial production in the corresponding sectors abroad and other commodity imports are related to UK domestic final expenditures.

Source: Barker (forthcoming).

price elasticity of -1.5. This means that there has to be a continual improvement in the price competitiveness of UK manufactures to offset the structural trend in manufacturing imports *even if UK real incomes and expenditures remain constant.*

Nothing like this phenomenon exists for exports of manufactures, which have an activity elasticity of only 0.8 and only a weak upward trend. However in comparison with other countries' trade (see, for example, Akhtar, 1981 and Goldstein and Khan, 1978) it is not that UK import elasticities are high but that UK export elasticities are exceptionally low, as is shown in Table 2.3. Although these elasticities are for total exports, since manufactures are more than half of exports they tend to reflect manufacturing performance.

Services is now the next-largest exporting and importing sector after manufacturing and here too there is a structural imbalance between exports and imports. The activity elasticity for imports of manufacturing is 3 to 4 times that of exports of manufacturing while the corresponding ratio for services is only 2. In addition, there is a strong negative trend

Table 2.3   *Cross-country comparison of export activity elasticities*

France	1.70
West Germany	2.07
Italy	2.10
UK	0.90
USA	1.02
Japan	3.67
Belgium	1.83
Netherlands	1.92

Source: Goldstein and Khan (1978), Table 4.

of 6 per cent p.a. for imports of services, arising from the decline in imports of sea-transport, distribution and business services.

There is no reason to believe that these structural parameters have shifted in recent years. As Table 2.4 shows, manufactured imports have continued to rise rapidly and manufactured exports have not kept pace with the growth in world trade. However, these changes are affected by the high value of sterling in 1978-83 and other adverse movements in price competitiveness, and a proper assessment of the evidence at disaggregated level is yet to be done.

Table 2.4   *Manufactures: world trade and UK exports and imports, 1980-85*

1980=100

	Volume of world trade in manufacturing	UK manufacturing exports	UK manufacturing imports
1980	100	100	100
1981	103	94	98
1982	100	96	107
1983	104	96	122
1984	114	104	134
1985	119	111	141

Source: *National Institute Economic Review*, May 1986 and CSO *Monthly Digest of Statistics*, March 1986.

The oil contribution to the balance of payments

North Sea oil has provided a very substantial flow of foreign-exchange resources, starting in the late 1970s and reaching a peak in 1985. Fig. 2.1 shows the balance of trade in oil together with the current account on the balance of payments 1974-87, with the last year being forecasts or current trends. The significance of the move from oil deficit to oil surplus is that this is a largely exogenous contribution to the balance of payments, arising from depleting a natural resource rather than from building up an export capacity of renewable assets.

Figure 2.1   *The balance of trade in oil and the balance of payments*

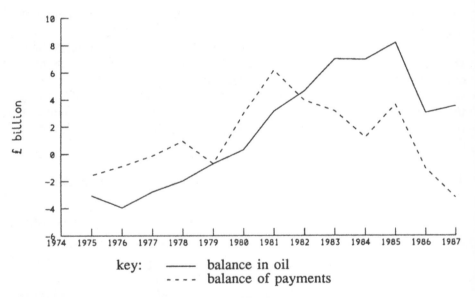

key: ——— balance in oil
         - - - - balance of payments

Source: UK CSO *Pink Book*, 1985; DTI Press Release, May 1986; CEF 1986/2.

The magnitude of this contribution should not be under-estimated. Although the net output of oil and gas is only some 7 per cent of GDP, most of it is tradeable and if it had to be imported then, even allowing for the net repayment of interest, profits and dividends on the foreign investment in exploration and production, the value of the imported oil and gas would have been £17.9 billion in 1984, representing 5.6 per cent of GDP at current market prices. To put this in perspective, the worst balance-of-payments deficit of the 1970s (and indeed of the whole of the post-war period) was in 1974, reaching 4.0 per cent of GDP.

Figure 2.2 *UK net identified external assets*

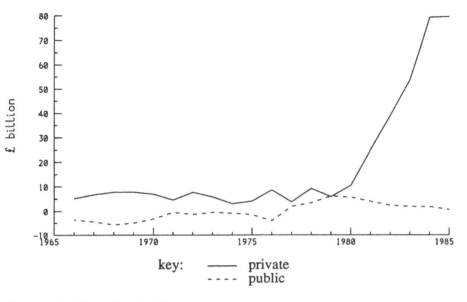

Source: UK CSO *Pink Book*, 1985.

The balance-of-payments surpluses have allowed a large accumulation of assets abroad following the relaxation of controls on the movement of financial capital in 1979. Fig. 2.2 shows private and public accumulation of net external assets up until 1985. The rise is dramatic, but it is almost all in private portfolios. This means that there is no guarantee that it will flow back into the UK when the balance of payments moves into deficit. Indeed, there is not even a strong reason why the income flows on these foreign investments should not be re-invested abroad. The situation today is fundamentally different from that before the First World War when there was also a large external surplus. Today the UK is a relatively small economy and the financial markets have expanded out of recognition. A rise in UK interest rates, especially in an attempt to draw in short-term finance to cover a current-account deficit, may well be interpreted by the market as a signal that the exchange rate is likely to depreciate, so that potential exchange-rate losses may outweigh interest-differential gains and finance will flow out of the country rather than into it.

Oil and manufacturing

Figure 2.3   *Shares of manufacturing and oil in GDP*

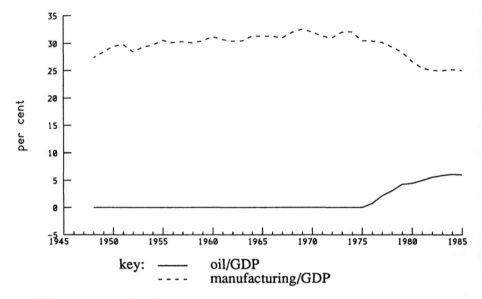

key: ——————   oil/GDP
       - - - -   manufacturing/GDP

Source: CSO *Monthly Digest of Statistics.*

Fig. 2.3 shows the shares of oil, gas and manufacturing (defined now in the SIC to include food manufactures) over the period of the build-up of North Sea oil and gas production, 1976-85. The rise in the oil share appears to be almost exactly reflected by a decline in the manufacturing share.

Before 1973 the manufacturing share had been rising about a trend. What is so notable about the decline in the share after 1973 is that manufacturing has taken all the burden of adjustment to the oil and gas increases even though it is less than 30 per cent of GDP. Since the oil industry employs a very small number of people compared with manufacturing, the implication of the adjustment is that large numbers of people become unemployed unless there is a sufficient increase in aggregate demand.

2.4 The prospects for UK trade and the balance of payments, 1987-2000

This section of the chapter summarises forecasts for the structure of trade and the balance of payments in the Cambridge Econometrics Post Budget Forecast of April 1987 (CEF87/2). The policy assumption behind the forecast is of a broad continuation of present policies with no major initiative to reduce unemployment.

The structure of trade

Table 2.5   *Sector shares^a in UK exports*

per cent

	1985	1990	1995	2000
Agriculture & other	2.7	2.5	2.3	2.0
Energy and water	17.6	13.0	7.5	5.0
Manufacturing^b	59.6	63.3	66.8	57.5
Services	20.1	21.2	23.4	25.6
Total	100.0	100.0	100.0	100.0

Notes: [a] The shares are calculated from constant-priced data.
     [b] Manufacturing includes food, drink and tobacco.
Source: Cambridge Econometrics *Forecast* 1987/2.

Table 2.5 shows the shares of 4 sectors of the economy in total exports every 5 years 1985-2000, excluding construction exports which are negligible. The major change is the fall in oil exports and therefore the fall in the energy export share throughout the period. Manufacturing rises from 60 per cent to 67 per cent of total exports and services increase from about 20 per cent 1985-90 to 26 per cent of the total by the end of the century. Thus the picture is of the rise in manufacturing and service exports compensating for the fall in oil exports.

Table 2.6 shows the comparable table for imports. There is not so much change here, with the manufactured import share rising slowly from 72 per cent in 1985 to 77 per cent in 2000. The services share is forecast to fall slightly.

Table 2.6   *Sector shares^a in UK imports*

per cent

	1985	1990	1995	2000
Agriculture & other	5.8	4.9	4.0	3.5
Energy and water	9.5	10.0	10.5	9.9
Manufacturing^b	72.0	74.0	75.2	77.0
Services	12.7	11.1	10.2	9.7
Total	100.0	100.0	100.0	100.0

Notes: ^{a}The shares are calculated from constant-priced data.
^{b}Manufacturing includes food, drink and tobacco.
Source: Cambridge Econometrics *Forecast* 1987/2.

The balance of payments

Table 2.7 shows each sector's net contribution to the balance of payments with the upper panel showing the values in £ billion and the lower panel showing the contribution as a percentage of GDP at current market prices.

The sectoral shifts are much more extreme than in the share tables (Tables 2.5 and 2.6) based on constant-priced data. In the forecast the exchange rate depreciates progressively as a reaction to the balance-of-payments deficits and this worsens the terms of trade, particularly for oil which is priced in dollars. The oil deficit appears by the year 1991 and moves to 2.1 per cent of GDP by the year 2000. The manufacturing deficit, already apparent by 1985, worsens until the early 1990s; however it is offset by a services surplus. The surplus of services is eventually large enough to bring the balance of payments back towards zero.

The exchange rate is prevented from depreciating even more quickly by high UK interest rates relative to the rest of the world from 1988 onwards. The interest payments on the capital inflows eventually become equal to the receipts of property income on the net foreign assets accumulated over the period 1979-85, and the net balance of property income and transfers is negligible by the year 2000.

Table 2.7   *Net sector balances in the balance of payments*

£ billion

	1985	1990	1995	2000
Agriculture & other	-3	-4	-5	-7
Energy and water	5	0	-10	-23
Manufacturing	9	-21	-26	-31
Services	9	15	36	66
Balance of trade	4	-10	-10	5
Property income & transfers	-1	2	2	0
Balance of payments	3	8	-8	5

per cent of GDP at market prices

	1985	1990	1995	2000
Agriculture & other	-0.9	-0.8	-0.7	-0.7
Energy and water	1.5	0.0	-1.3	-2.1
Manufacturing	-2.6	-4.3	-3.5	-2.9
Services	2.6	3.1	4.8	6.2
Balance of trade	1.0	-2.0	-1.3	0.4
Property income & transfers	-0.3	0.4	0.3	0.0
Balance of payments	1.0	-1.1	-1.6	0.4

Note: Valuation is on the basis of the CSO's *Commodity Flow Accounts.*
Source: Cambridge Econometrics *Forecast* 1987/2.

Energy, manufacturing and services

Figs 2.4, 2.5 and 2.6 show the shares in exports, imports, domestic demand and gross output for each of the main sectors discussed in this chapter. They summarise the implications of the forecast for the sectors.

The energy sector includes coal, gas and electricity as well as oil and hence its share in total gross output falls quite slowly. The main feature of the chart relating to this sector is the fall in the export share. The manufacturing sector holds its export share and its share of domestic demand, but imports take more and more of this demand. The service sector shows a strong growth in the share of exports and gross output, since imports grow less than proportionately with demand. However, much of the growth in gross output is in intermediate sales of services, such as communications services sold to business and distribution. The growth in net output of services is appreciably less than that in gross output.

Figure 2.4 *Energy and water*

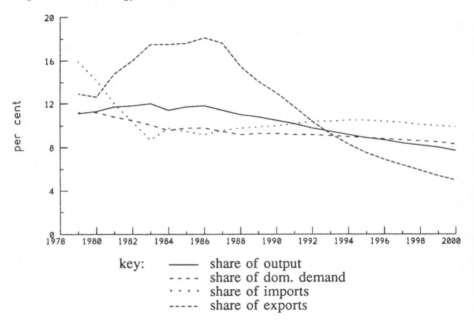

key: ———   share of output
         - - - -   share of dom. demand
         · · · ·   share of imports
         - - - - -   share of exports

Source: UK CSO *Commodity Flow Accounts*, 1985; CEF 1986/2.

Figure 2.5   *Manufacturing*

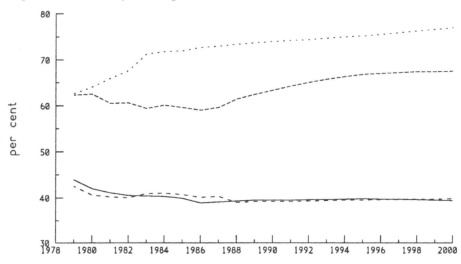

Figure 2.6   *Services*

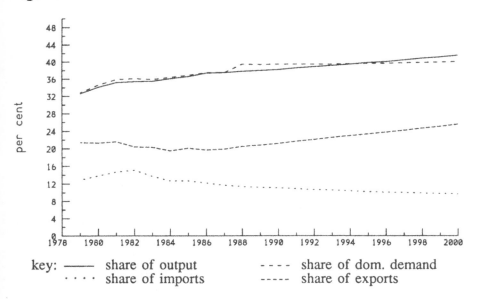

key: —— share of output   - - - - share of dom. demand
     · · · · share of imports   - - - - - share of exports

Source: UK CSO *Commodity Flow Accounts*, 1985; CEF 1986/2.

2.5 Policies for the balance of payments and their effects on manufacturing and services

This section examines two policies which tend to improve the balance of payments and at the same time reduce unemployment. These are exchange-rate depreciation, via lower UK interest rates relative to US interest rates, and a formal prices and incomes policy. Deflationary policies such as further government spending cuts or increases in taxes may also improve the balance of payments, but they are not considered here.

Exchange-rate depreciation

Table 2.8 *The effects of an exchange-rate depreciation of 10 per cent in 1986 on key economic indicators using MDM6*

	Growth in GDP	Inflation	BP/GDP	PSBR/GDP	Unemployment
	percentage point difference from base				thousands
1986	1.5	3.9	-0.8	-0.1	-90
1987	0.2	2.2	0.4	-0.4	-160
1988	-0.5	1.1	0.6	-0.4	-170
1990	-0.1	0.5	0.5	-0.4	-160
2000	0.0	0.9	0.1	-0.2	-100

Table 2.8 shows the effects of a 10 per cent depreciation in 1986 on the main economic indicators. There is a first-year impact on growth of 1.5 percentage points (p.p.) and on inflation of 3.9 p.p., and a noticeable J-curve effect on the balance of payments. However, the balance of payments improves from 1987 onwards, though this diminishes through time. The PSBR ratio is reduced because the higher growth generates more tax revenues although these are offset by higher costs of goods and services bought by the public sector. Unemployment is reduced by 90,000 in the first year, 160,000 in the second and 170,000 in the third.

The effects on exports, imports, the balance of trade and gross output of manufactures and services are shown in Table 2.9. The depreciation increases exports of manufactures more than those of services and since the absolute levels of manufactures are also higher than those of services there is a distinct shift towards manufactured exports. At the same time, after an initial expansion, manufactured imports fall below base levels, although this is not enough to prevent adverse terms-of-trade effects producing deficits in the balance of trade in manufactures. These deficits are more than offset by surpluses in services trade giving an overall surplus. Depreciation tends to shift more output into manufacturing, reflecting the fact that the sector produces a more tradeable output.

Table 2.9   *The effects of an exchange-rate depreciation of 10 per cent in 1986 on trade in manufactures and services using MDM6*

	Exports		Imports		Balance of Trade			Gross Output	
	Manu. %	Services %	Manu. %	Services %	Manu. £bn	Services £bn	Total £bn	Manu. %	Services %
1986	2.3	2.7	1.3	1.5	-3	1	-2	2.5	1.4
1987	3.2	2.6	0.2	2.1	-1	2	1	3.2	1.5
1988	2.3	2.1	-0.8	0.8	0	2	2	2.3	1.1
1990	1.6	1.5	-0.8	0.0	0	3	3	1.6	0.7
2000	0.5	0.8	-0.1	0.1	-7	11	2	0.8	0.5

An incomes policy

An incomes policy tends to have more favourable effects than exchange-rate depreciation because it improves competitiveness by reducing average earnings and prices. It is modelled in MDM by a dummy variable in the average-earnings equation (see Lawson, forthcoming), the variable being derived from an analysis of the effects of various incomes policies which have been tried in the past. The dummy variable has a value of 4.5 for 1977, a time of strong incomes policies, and 1 for various years when there was a weak incomes policy. The simulation of the effects of an incomes policy from 1986 assumes a weak policy and it is modelled by adding 1 to the incomes policy dummy in the base projection. An important assumption made in this simulation is that the exchange rate is prevented from appreciating in response to the lower domestic inflation.

Table 2.10 shows the main macroeconomic effects. Growth in GDP is initially reduced as nominal incomes are lower, but this is a small temporary effect. Inflation is lower throughout and the balance of

Table 2.10[a] *The effects of a 'weak'[b] incomes policy from 1986 on key economic indicators using MDM6*

	Growth in GDP	Inflation	BP/GDP	PSBR/GDP	Unemployment
	percentage point difference from base				thousands
1986	-0.2	-0.7	0.3	-0.0	-30
1987	0.1	-0.8	0.4	-0.1	-70
1988	0.1	-0.6	0.4	-0.2	-110
1990	0.1	-0.3	0.5	-0.4	-190
2000	0.0	-0.1	0.6	-0.7	-350

Notes: [a] This simulation assumes that the exchange rate is held at base levels and not allowed to appreciate.

[b] A 'weak' incomes policy is one which increases the 'strength-of-incomes-policy' dummy variable in the average-earnings equation by 1. See Lawson (forthcoming).

payments improves to a greater extent than it does with a sterling depreciation. The PSBR ratio to GDP is lower and unemployment is brought down by an increasing amount.

All in all this is a very favourable set of results: the problem is that incomes policies have been discredited by the argument that their effects are at best temporary. The results with MDM confirm that an incomes policy of some sort is one of the few measures available to ease the balance-of-payments constraint on growth and employment without generating renewed inflation.

Table 2.11 shows the effects of incomes policy on manufacturing and services. With no adverse terms-of-trade effect, it is now manufacturing which produces the largest net surpluses on the balance of trade. The negligible effect of the policy on growth means that the improved competitiveness has maximum effects on imports of manufactures. One interesting feature is the reduction in services' gross output below base: this is a result of the reallocation of expenditures away from consumption with a higher-than-average services content towards international trade with a lower services content.

Table 2.11   *The effects of a 'weak' incomes policy from 1986 on trade in manufactures and services using MDM6*

	Exports		Imports		Balance of Trade			Gross Output	
	Man. %	Services %	Manu. %	Services %	Manu. £bn	Services £bn	Total £bn	Manu. %	Services %
1986	0.1	0.1	-1.0	-0.7	1	0	1	0.1	-0.2
1987	0.4	0.3	-1.2	-0.8	1	0	1	0.4	-0.2
1988	0.6	0.6	-1.1	-0.6	1	0	2	0.6	-0.1
1990	0.9	1.1	-1.0	-0.3	2	1	4	0.8	0.1
2000	1.0	1.8	-0.7	-0.1	4	3	7	0.9	0.5

Notes: See Table 4.3.
Source: Cambridge Econometrics *Forecast* 1986/2 and this chapter.

Conclusion

The effects of depreciation and incomes policy illustrate how manufacturing and services might react to market forces (depreciation) or government policies (incomes policy) which ease the balance-of-payments constraint. In both cases manufacturing rises as a share of output, but its net contribution to the balance of payments is negative with depreciation and positive with incomes policy. Services exports play a key role in improving the balance of trade after a depreciation of sterling.

2.6 Manufactures or services?

This section returns to the debate at the start of the chapter. From the disaggregated analysis, it is clear that there are strong interdependencies between manufacturing and services and that contributions to the balance of payments are likely to come from both sectors depending on circumstances.

However, it seems very likely that the economy will become severely constrained by the balance of payments in the next year or so, making the reduction of unemployment (let alone the achievement of full employment) virtually impossible under present policies without unacceptable inflation. Therefore any policies which improve the performance of domestic industries, whether manufacturing or services, are worth considering, especially if they take time to have effect.

Services, particularly financial services, have been making an increasing contribution to the balance of payments, with real exports rising by 11.8 per cent p.a. 1974-85 but real imports rising by only 2.9 per cent p.a. This performance needs to be maintained, for example by further pressure on the UK's EEC partners to liberalise their financial markets. On the supply side, more education and training in financial skills are called for to keep the UK sector competitive. The City has become one of the main centres for cost and wage inflation in the UK and this inflation could threaten future expansion.

The structural weakness of manufacturing has long been the subject of debate, with the House of Lords Report providing the latest list of recommendations for action. A common theme is the low level of investment but to put this right would mean an unprecedented inflow of private or public finance to industries which have scope for economies of scale and specialisation in world markets. However, the employment requirements of manufacturing are likely to fall even further because new equipment is so productive. It is the service industries, particularly social services in health and education, which provide the most scope for increasing employment.

3

MANUFACTURING AND SERVICES IN UK MACRO-MODELS

John Whitley

3.1 Introduction

This chapter compares and contrasts the approaches to, and the consequences of, disaggregation in the main UK macroeconomic models. The models considered are those that were deposited at the ESRC Macroeconomic Modelling Bureau at the University of Warwick in late 1985 or early 1986. The models are those of the Cambridge Growth Project (CGP), the City University Business School (CUBS), the Bank of England (BE), the London Business School (LBS), the National Institute of Economic and Social Research (NIESR), the Liverpool Research Group in Macroeconomics (LPL), and Her Majesty's Treasury (HMT).

There has been some concern in recent years over the alleged relative weakness of the manufacturing sector of the economy and this has been heightened by the phenomenon known as the 'Dutch disease'. According to the proponents of this theory, the exploitation of major new oil reserves has been the cause of a substantial decline in the manufacturing base owing to adverse shifts in the terms of trade. The Dutch disease is often associated loosely with de-industralisation which is usually defined as a permanent loss of manufacturing capacity. A key factor in this de-industrialisation process is the response of the exchange rate to the discovery of oil reserves (which causes an appreciation of the exchange rate) and hence a loss of international competitiveness. A more detailed discussion of the Dutch disease and the impact of North Sea oil in relation to the UK macroeconomic models is given in Wallis (ed.) (1985). Given that the macro-models now include the decline in the UK manufacturing base as part of their sample experience it is of interest to examine the extent to which a bias in favour of the service sector relative to manufacturing is built into the simulation properties of these models. In Section 3.2 of this chapter, the extent of disaggregation in the UK models is outlined and the methods used to derive sectoral output and employment are described. Section 3.3 examines the impact on sectoral output and employment derived by applying a set of common macroeconomic shocks to the models. It is found that the sectoral responses depend on both the nature of the shock and on the particular model chosen. Section 3.4 considers the extent to which the models are useful for handling policy changes, which are themselves disaggregated in nature, and draws some conclusions regarding the applicability of UK models to policy questions.

3.2 Disaggregation in UK models

The first part of this section describes the extent of disaggregation in the models and this is followed by an account of the methods used to derive sectoral output and employment. Focus on disaggregation enables some conclusions to be drawn from the issues discussed earlier.

The extent of disaggregation

In general, disaggregation is very limited in the UK models. The LPL model analyses the economy as a whole and there is no disaggregation at all. Thus, for example, there is no special treatment even for the oil sector, since it is argued that efficient markets adjust for the development (and later disappearance) of a domestic oil sector, with no overall impact on the level of activity and prices. The CUBS model is much more of a non-market-clearing model and treats separately the oil sector, the traded goods sector, public utilities, dwellings and government. The price of oil is largely determined by world markets and the output of oil is exogenous. Output and employment in the government sector are derived from exogenous assumptions concerning the growth of public expenditure, and output and employment in public utilities are determined by total output in the economy. The relevant behavioural relationships in the model are those of output and employment in the traded goods sector.

At the other extreme is the CGP model, where the economy is separated into 39 different industrial activities, each with its own accounting framework. In between we have the four quarterly models,

LBS, NIESR, HMT and BE, which adopt a similar level of disaggregation. All distinguish the oil sector, manufacturing, and general government. LBS, HMT and BE then have a residual sector which is called non-manufacturing and includes the service sector, agriculture, coal mining, construction and public utilities. Agriculture and public utilities are defined separately in the NIESR model but output in these sectors is taken to be exogenous. Consequently, the main sectors whose behaviour is described by the model are manufacturing and non-manufacturing. This appears to be the lowest common denominator in the models and is the disaggregation we use in the following analysis. For convenience we sometimes refer to non-manufacturing as the service sector but it should be borne in mind that it includes agriculture, public utilities and construction in addition to the usual service-sector industries.

Given the limited degree of disaggregation in the CUBS and LPL models, they are not included in the further analysis. Not all analysis is conducted consistently at a disaggregated level within the models. For example, the LBS model does not treat manufacturing and non-manufacturing investment separately, nor is the principal behavioural equation for imports broken down in this way. Only aggregate earnings are distinguished in the NIESR model and in general price disaggregation relates only to manufactured goods. A distinctive feature of the latest version of the NIESR model is the disaggregation of the employment-unemployment relationship where labour in the manufacturing sector is assumed to have a lower propensity to register as unemployed than labour in non-manufacturing.

Approaches to disaggregation

In most of the models, where disaggregation occurs it is usually as a matter of convenience or necessity. Thus we observe that not all components of the manufacturing or non-manufacturing sectors are modelled consistently. However, in the CGP model disaggregation is a methodological issue. Although there are some aggregate relationships, such as consumer spending and wages, the essence of the approach is to derive both sectoral output and the level of GDP by summation over the individual industries. Each industry is modelled separately using behavioural relationships and accounting identities. Relationships between sectors through intermediate demand flows are derived by input-output analysis.

In contrast, the other models ignore intermediate demand and determine net rather than gross output. Sectoral output is derived by breaking down GDP into constituent parts (the top-down approach) whereas the CGP model builds up GDP from its constituents (the bottom-up approach). The LBS, NIESR and HMT models use input-output weights and the expenditure components of GDP to calculate the level of output in the manufacturing sector. Fixed weights are used (taken from a particular input-output table) so that the assumption is that the marginal weight of manufacturing in total consumption, say, is equal to the average weight. Manufacturing output then typically drives employment, investment and stockbuilding in the models so that the manufacturing output relationship plays a simultaneous rather than purely recursive role. It should be noted that very aggregate expenditure items often enter into the manufacturing output relationship, so that although the models separate out consumer durables from non-durables, for example, the information gain from allowing for a different contribution to manufacturing output is not always exploited in the output relationship (e.g. LBS, NIESR).

The particular weights chosen for the LBS equation (see Table 3.1) which are also typical of those for NIESR and HMT, imply that manufacturing output only increases by 0.4 per cent if all the expenditure elements (and hence GDP) each increase by 1 per cent. Thus there is a built-in tendency in the models for balanced expansion to be relatively detrimental to the manufacturing sector. The nature of the weights also implies that expenditure has to be biased towards stockbuilding or net trade (exports less imports) in order for manufacturing output to sustain its share in GDP. However, imports are far more sensitive to domestic demand than are exports so that there has to be some gain in price or non-price competitiveness in order for an improvement in net trade to be achieved.

An important difference between the NIESR and HMT models is that the NIESR model allocates all of imports and exports of manufactures to the manufacturing sector, but the HMT model allocates only two-thirds of this trade to manufacturing. The LBS model relates manufacturing output only to total imports and exports. The relatively low weight on fixed investment in manufacturing output in the models reflects the role of investment in buildings which determines construction sector output and is included in non-manufacturing. Output in non-manufacturing in all these models is derived as a residual given GDP and manufacturing output.

The BE model allocates GDP to manufacturing and non-manufacturing through a two-stage approach. In the first stage, the total demand for manufactures is calculated using a weighting method similar to that of the other models but ignoring the import contribution and exploiting some of the other disaggregated information in the model. In the second stage, the share of imports in total demand is derived from

Table 3.1   *The determination of manufacturing output in the models*

	LBS	NIESR	Weights on expenditure variables HMT	BE
Consumption	0.198	0.195	0.131 (total) 0.302 (clothing+durables) 0.143 (food,drink,tobacco)	0.23 (non-durables) 0.9 (durables)
Government current expenditure	0.328[a]	0.170	0.347[a]	0.18
Fixed investment	0.386	0.390	0.31 0.28 (plant,machinery)	0.6 (priv. non-hsng) 0.3 (priv. housing) 0.47 (govt non-hsng) 0.44 (govt housing)
Stockbuilding	0.600	0.660		0.6 (mats+fuel) 0.9 (distributors) 0.6 (other)
Exports	0.436	1.0 (manuf.)	0.65 (manuf.)	1.0 (manuf.) 0.9 (other)
Imports	-0.296	-1.0 (manuf.)	-0.654 (manuf.)	
Factor cost adjustment	-0.230	-		

Note: [a] Procurement.

an equation which has relative prices as one of its determinants. Thus here the share of imports is explicitly modelled, whereas it is implicit in the other models which embody an increasing import share given that imports have an elasticity of greater than unity with respect to final demand.

Employment at the sectoral level is determined largely by the level of output but most of the models contain some allowance for the impact of real wages on employment (see Table 3.2). Real wages have the greatest influence for manufacturing in the NIESR model, followed by LBS. However there is no real wage influence on non-manufacturing in the NIESR model and the LBS real-wage elasticity is far greater than that in the other models. The long-run output elasticities are all close to unity, the main exception being NIESR where, in addition, it is expected output that drives employment and output expectations from a forward

Table 3.2   *Employment relationships in the models. Long-run elasticities*

	Real wages		Output	
	Manuf.	Non-manuf.	Manuf.	Non-manuf.
CGP	-0.41	-0.32	0.97	0.98
LBS	-0.73	-1.10	0.84	1.0
BE	-0.05	-0.10	1.0	1.0
HMT	-0.33	-0.11	1.0	1.0
NIESR	-1.3	-	1.8	0.6

consistent expectations approach. The BE employment equation for manufacturing is specified in terms of man-hours but terms in hours of work only appear explicitly in the CGP model.

3.3 Simulation results

We now examine the responses of output and employment in manufacturing and non-manufacturing in the simulation experiments. For the CGP model these are computed by aggregating across the relevant 23 industrial sectors to give a manufacturing total, taking non-manufacturing as the aggregation of the remaining 15 non-oil sectors. We analyse the results in two ways. First, we consider the results from each model in order to see whether different exogenous shocks have different sectoral implications and, second, we analyse the results across the models in order to observe whether sectoral effects differ between models for the same exogenous shock.

Five exogenous shocks are chosen to illustrate the properties of the models. Three of the shocks relate to fiscal policy, one to monetary policy and the remaining shock to external developments. The three fiscal shocks are a permanent increase in government current expenditure of £1600m p.a. at 1980 prices, balanced equally between procurement and employment-related expenditure; a permanent reduction of 5 per cent in the standard rate of income tax (e.g. from 30 to 28.5 per cent); and a reduction of 10 per cent in the rate of VAT (e.g. from 15 to 13.5 per cent). The monetary shock is a permanent reduction of 2 percentage points in the short-term interest rate. The external shock is a permanent 10 per cent reduction in the world dollar price of oil. In this final simulation all other world variables are assumed to be unchanged. This simulation should therefore be regarded as a sensitivity exercise on the models, rather than a plausible account of the interaction between oil prices and world activity. (Simulations which are of this scenario-setting type are discussed in Powell and Horton, 1985.) In the fiscal simulations the changes in expenditure and taxation are assumed to be financed under the assumption of constant interest rates. This is roughly equivalent to assuming money finance of the resulting deficit.

We first look at the results by model. These results are shown in Tables 3.3-3.7. Given that the non-manufacturing sector is somewhat larger than the manufacturing sector we give employment responses in both absolute and percentage deviations from the base run.

Simulations with the LBS model

We turn first to the results from the LBS model (Table 3.3). In the government expenditure simulation there is an implicit increase in the output of the public sector; consequently, both manufacturing and non-manufacturing output increase by less than GDP. The rise in manufacturing output is greater than that in non-manufacturing initially, as the sharp fall in the real exchange rate (see Table 3.8) boosts net trade, which is favourable to manufacturing output. After five years, however, the initial impetus weakens and the differential output effect is considerably less. Employment in manufacturing is still adjusting to the peak effect on output after five years, so that the balance of employment effects continues to favour manufacturing. In terms of absolute effects on employment the difference between sectors is negligible, however.

The exchange rate adjustment in the income tax simulation also favours manufacturing output, with a peaked reaction similar to that for the government expenditure simulation. Here the manufacturing employment response is somewhat greater relative to that of output by the end of the simulation but, although the percentage response of manufacturing employment is almost twice that of non-manufacturing after five years, there is yet again little difference between relative employment effects when measured as deviations in the numbers employed.

Even though the scale of GDP effects differs between the simulations, there is a pronounced tendency for the impact to favour manufacturing output relative to non-manufacturing. This is not surprising given that the exchange rate falls in each case and thus gives a (temporary) boost to net trade. The relative impact is weakest for the VAT and oil price simulations where the decline in the exchange rate is more modest than in the other simulations.

The relative proportional employment responses largely follow from those of output with the exception of the VAT experiment. The fall in

Table 3.3 *Sectoral output and employment effects - LBS model (differences from base run)*

Year	OUTPUT %			EMPLOYMENT %		000s	
	GDP	Manuf.	Non-manuf.	Manuf.	Non-manuf.	Manuf.	Non-manuf.
Government expenditure[a]							
1	0.7	0.4	0.3	0.2	0.1	13	10
3	1.0	0.9	0.5	0.9	0.4	48	47
5	1.0	0.8	0.7	1.3	0.5	71	55
Income tax rate[b]							
1	0.2	0.3	0.3	0.2	0.1	13	9
3	0.7	1.0	0.7	1.1	0.5	57	60
5	0.7	0.8	0.9	1.5	0.8	84	90
VAT[c]							
1	0.2	0.3	0.3	0.2	0.1	13	12
3	0.4	0.6	0.3	0.7	0.7	38	84
5	0.2	0.2	0.3	0.5	0.9	29	106
Interest rates[d]							
1	0.7	1.0	0.8	0.6	0.3	32	30
3	1.3	2.0	1.3	2.1	1.5	116	179
5	0.8	1.1	0.9	2.1	1.6	111	201
Oil prices[e]							
1	0.3	0.3	0.3	-0.1	0.1	-5	8
3	0.5	0.8	0.3	0.6	0.4	35	43
5	0.3	0.4	0.4	0.8	0.4	42	48

Notes: [a] Increase of £1600m p.a. (1980 prices) in current expenditure, money finance, balanced equally between procurement and employment.
[b] Reduction of 5% (from 30 to 28.8%).
[c] Reduction of 10% (from 15 to 13.5%).
[d] Reduction of 2 percentage points in short-term interest rates.
[e] Reduction of 10% in world dollar prices.

manufacturing employment in the oil price simulation occurs as a result of the change in price of inputs relative to the output price in manufacturing. In both the VAT and interest rate simulations the absolute deviations of employment are far greater for non-manufacturing than for manufacturing. The LBS sectoral results therefore reflect the macroeconomic responses, and in particular the exchange rate adjustment. Given that this has a primary effect on net trade, output in the manufacturing sector is affected to a greater extent than non-manufacturing output.

Simulations with the NIESR model

Table 3.4   *Sectoral output and employment effects - NIESR model (differences from base run)*

Year	OUTPUT %			EMPLOYMENT %		000s	
	GDP	Manuf.	Non-manuf.	Manuf.	Non-manuf.	Manuf.	Non-manuf.
Government expenditure[a]							
1	0.7	0.6	0.1	0.1	-	6	3
3	0.7	0.6	-	0.2	0.1	10	7
5	0.6	0.5	-0.1	-0.1	-	-6	3
Income tax rate[b]							
1	0.1	0.2	0.4	0.1	0.2	4	14
3	0.4	0.4	0.6	0.2	0.8	12	72
5	0.4	0.5	0.6	-0.1	1.4	-4	134
VAT[c]							
1	0.2	0.2	0.3	0.1	0.1	7	11
3	0.3	0.3	0.5	0.7	0.6	36	55
5	0.3	0.4	0.5	0.7	1.2	39	109
Interest rates[d]							
1	0.1	0.2	-	0.1	-	7	1
3	0.1	0.1	0.1	0.2	0.1	13	8
5	-	0.1	-	0.1	0.1	4	9
Oil prices[e]							
1	-	0.1	-	-	-	2	1
3	0.1	0.2	0.1	0.2	0.1	11	11
5	0.1	0.3	0.1	0.2	0.3	13	25

Notes: [a] Increase of £1600m p.a. (1980 prices) in current expenditure, money finance, balanced equally between procurement and employment.
[b] Reduction of 5% (from 30 to 28.8%).
[c] Reduction of 10% (from 15 to 13.5%).
[d] Reduction of 2 percentage points in short-term interest rates.
[e] Reduction of 10% in world dollar prices.

The comparable NIESR results are given in Table 3.4. In the absence of the same strength of exchange rate reaction in this model (see Table 3.8), the effects on output are not so biased towards manufacturing as in the LBS model. Indeed, a marked bias of this kind only appears in the government expenditure simulation. In the income tax simulation output effects are strongest in the service sector as consumers' expenditure and investment are boosted. The other simulations produce a balanced efect on sectoral outputs.

The response of non-manufacturing employment is greater than that of output in the income tax and VAT simulations. In the latter, for example, employment is 1.25 per cent higher after 5 years compared with an increase in output of 0.5 per cent. This may reflect the dynamics in the equation since the long-run output elasticity is only 0.6 (compared to the equivalent elasticity of 1.5 for manufacturing).

Simulations with the Treasury model

Sectoral effects for the HMT model are shown in Table 3.5. Here the impact on manufacturing output is at best equal to that of non-manufacturing, but is often weaker. In particular the VAT simulation is biased more towards non-manufacturing output. This is a consquence of increased expenditure on consumption and investment goods. There is greater variation in the output-employment response across sectors for this model, however. In several simulations the proportional response of non-manufacturing is weaker than that of manufacturing despite a stronger relative output effect. This is most apparent in the VAT and interest rate simulations. It does not seem possible to explain this feature in terms of real-wage movements, given that real wages rise in both simulations and that the real-wage elasticity is higher for manufacturing than for non-manufacturing. Nevertheless, the absolute increase of employment in non-manufacturing consistently exceeds that in manufacturing in the simulations with this model.

Table 3.5 *Sectoral output and employment effects - HMT model (differences from base run)*

Year	OUTPUT %			EMPLOYMENT %		000s	
	GDP	Manuf.	Non-manuf.	Manuf.	Non-manuf.	Manuf.	Non-manuf.
Government expenditure[a]							
1	0.7	0.2	0.3	0.1	0.1	6	15
3	0.7	0.3	0.4	0.3	0.2	15	35
5	0.5	0.1	0.2	-	-0.1	-2	-9
Income tax rate[b]							
1	0.2	0.2	0.2	0.1	0.1	3	10
3	0.3	0.4	0.4	0.5	0.4	25	56
5	0.3	0.4	0.5	0.6	0.5	31	71
VAT[c]							
1	0.3	0.2	0.4	-	0.1	2	12
3	0.6	0.5	0.8	0.7	0.7	37	101
5	0.7	0.5	1.0	1.0	0.9	48	135
Interest rates[d]							
1	0.6	0.8	0.7	0.2	0.1	13	16
3	1.5	1.7	1.9	1.7	0.9	89	138
5	1.3	1.3	1.8	1.6	0.5	78	74
Oil prices[e]							
1	0.1	0.1	0.1	-	-	-	1
3	0.2	0.2	0.2	0.1	0.2	6	23
5	0.1	0.1	0.1	-0.5	-	-26	7

Notes: [a] Increase of £1600m p.a. (1980 prices) in current expenditure, money finance, balanced equally between procurement and employment.
[b] Reduction of 5% (from 30 to 28.8%).
[c] Reduction of 10% (from 15 to 13.5%).
[d] Reduction of 2 percentage points in short-term interest rates.
[e] Reduction of 10% in world dollar prices.

Simulations with the Bank of England model

Results for the BE model are shown in Table 3.6. It is more difficult to discern relative sectoral differences from this model since the scale of GDP effects is much smaller than for the other models. There does appear to be a tendency towards a higher manufacturing output response throughout the simulations however, and this translates directly into employment. In some cases this implies a greater absolute increase of employment in manufacturing than in non-manufacturing, contrary to the

Table 3.6 *Sectoral output and employment effects - BE model (differences from base run)*

Year	OUTPUT %			EMPLOYMENT %		000s	
	GDP	Manuf.	Non-manuf.	Manuf.	Non-manuf.	Manuf.	Non-manuf.
Government expenditure[a]							
1	0.6	0.3	0.2	0.1	0.1	7	10
3	0.7	0.6	0.2	0.4	0.1	23	24
5							
Income tax rate[b]							
1	0.1	0.1	0.2	0.1	0.1	3	8
3	0.3	0.5	0.3	0.4	0.3	21	39
5							
VAT[c]							
1	0.1	0.2	0.1	0.1	0.1	4	9
3	0.2	0.4	0.2	0.4	0.2	21	28
5							
Interest rates[d]							
1	0.1	0.2	-	0.1	-	8	-3
3	-	-	-	0.5	-	29	1
5							
Oil prices[e]							
1	-	-	-	-	-	1	-1
3	0.1	0.2	-	0.1	-0.1	7	-6
5							

Notes: [a] Increase of £1600m p.a. (1980 prices) in current expenditure, money finance, balanced equally between procurement and employment.
[b] Reduction of 5% (from 30 to 28.8%).
[c] Reduction of 10% (from 15 to 13.5%).
[d] Reduction of 2 percentage points in short-term interest rates.
[e] Reduction of 10% in world dollar prices.

experience of the other models.

Simulations with the CGP model

Finally, we turn to the results for the CGP model (Table 3.7). Here we observe a fall in manufacturing output in several of the simulations. This occurs largely where the exchange rate appreciates in response to an exogenous shock (the reverse of the LBS case). Thus trade performance is weakened and this adversely affects the manufacturing

Table 3.7 *Sectoral output and employment effects - CGP model (differences from base run)*

Year	OUTPUT %			EMPLOYMENT %		000s	
	GDP	Manuf.	Non-manuf.	Manuf.	Non-manuf.	Manuf.	Non-manuf.
Government expenditure[a]							
1	0.6	-0.3	0.2	-0.1	0.1	-3	15
3	0.5	-0.2	0.3	-	0.2	-	34
5	0.6	-0.2	0.3	0.1	0.3	4	43
Income tax rate[b]							
1	0.2	0.1	0.2	0.4	0.3	23	38
3	0.1	-0.1	0.2	0.6	0.5	31	68
5	0.2	-	0.1	0.8	0.6	44	92
VAT[c]							
1	0.2	0.2	0.2	0.4	0.2	22	27
3	-0.3	-0.9	-0.3	-0.1	-	-8	6
5	-0.2	-0.6	-0.3	-	0.1	-2	14
Interest rates[d]							
1	-	0.1	0.1	0.1	-	5	-
3	-0.2	-0.4	-0.2	-0.2	-0.1	-10	-7
5	-0.1	-0.2	-0.1	-0.3	-0.1	-14	-14
Oil prices[e]							
1	-	0.2	-	-	-	2	3
3	1.3	2.9	1.3	2.1	0.9	120	119
5	0.4	0.9	0.5	1.7	0.6	90	89

Notes: [a] Increase of £1600m p.a. (1980 prices) in current expenditure, money finance, balanced equally between procurement and employment.
[b] Reduction of 5% (from 30 to 28.8%).
[c] Reduction of 10% (from 15 to 13.5%).
[d] Reduction of 2 percentage points in short-term interest rates.
[e] Reduction of 10% in world dollar prices.

sector. Only in one case, the oil price simulation, does manufacturing output improve more (or deteriorate less) than that of non-manufacturing, and here the exchange rate declines sharply. In general, therefore, the proportionate employment responses are weaker for manufacturing relative to non-manufacturing in this model and hence the absolute increase in manufacturing employment is considerably smaller than that in non-manufacturing.

Table 3.8   *Exchange-rate effects in the simulations (% difference from base run)*

Year	LBS	NIESR	HMT	BE	CGP
Government current expenditure increase					
1	-3.7	-0.3	-0.4	-0.1	-
3	-4.9	-1.0	-1.9	-1.1	-0.1
5	-6.6	-2.0	-3.3	-	-
Income tax reduction					
1	-3.9	-0.3	-0.4	-	1.6
3	-5.4	-0.5	-1.4	-0.3	1.3
5	-7.3	-1.2	-2.2	-	1.9
VAT reduction					
1	-2.9	-0.3	-	-	5.1
3	-2.6	-0.3	-0.7	-0.4	3.9
5	-3.4	-0.4	-1.5	-	4.5
Interest rate reduction					
1	-7.6	-0.6	-3.4	-0.1	1.4
3	-7.7	-0.2	-6.2	-0.6	1.2
5	-9.3	-0.1	-8.1	0.8	-
World oil price reduction					
1	-3.5	-0.4	-1.4	-	-
3	-2.6	-0.3	-1.9	-0.1	-6.3
5	-2.6	-0.4	-1.9	-	-3.6

Summary of the employment responses

We can summarise the sectoral results so far as follows. The LBS model tends to favour the manufacturing sector in terms of output across the simulations, mainly on account of the exchange-rate depreciation in this model. This favours manufacturing through the trade response. In contrast, the CGP results favour non-manufacturing output in general since the exchange-rate adjustment is the reverse of that for LBS. The NIESR and HMT simulations tend to produce a more balanced output effect across the sectors since the composition of final expenditure changes is more evenly balanced than for LBS or for CGP. However, the relative employment responses differ in that for NIESR the response is stronger for non-manufacturing employment than for output, with the reverse occurring for HMT.

There is a clear contrast between both the extent and method of disaggregation in the CGP model and those in the other models. In aggregating over the 39 industries of the CGP model to obtain the sectoral estimates we lose some of the richness of information given by the individual industrial responses. Some quite marked compositional effects are present within these aggregate sectors in the simulations. Taking the VAT simulation as an example, the aggregate fall in manufacturing output after 5 years is 0.6 per cent and for non-manufacturing it is 0.3 per cent. Within manufacturing the range is from +0.7 per cent to -4.0 per cent, however, and within non-manufacturing +0.2 per cent to -4.1 per cent. Similar effects are also observed in the other simulations.

In summary we can say that, in terms of the absolute employment response, the LBS model produces the largest differential in favour of non-manufacturing for the VAT and interest rate simulations and that this is supported by the HMT results. The NIESR simulations reveal that the income tax and VAT reductions induce the greatest differential in favour of non-manufacturing employment and the CGP model produces this effect for the income tax simulation. The differential employment effects are all small for BE, with the most pronounced effect once again occurring for the income tax simulation. The LBS model gives the largest impact on manufacturing sector employment in the income tax simulations and the NIESR model the smallest. The former arises from the exchange-rate decline, whereas the weakness of the NIESR result is due to the employment response relative to that of output. In contrast the CGP model has a weak output but stronger employment reaction.

There is less discrepancy between the estimates of the impact on non-manufacturing employment in the income tax case. For the VAT simulation the main difference is between the responses of BE and CGP and the other models. The exchange rate rise leads to a fall in output in both sectors for CGP.

A comparison of the results

We now turn to a comparison of the results across the models, concentrating on the employment responses. These are shown in Figs 3.1-3.5.

The government spending simulation. For the government spending simulation the LBS model generates the largest employment response in manufacturing and CGP the least. The other three models (BE, HMT, and NIESR) all have similar profiles and fairly comparable estimates of the employment effect. The more divergent LBS result can be explained as a result of the sharp decline in the exchange rate in this model,

Figure 3.1 *Government spending simulation*

(a) effects on employment in manufacturing - differences from base run (thousands)

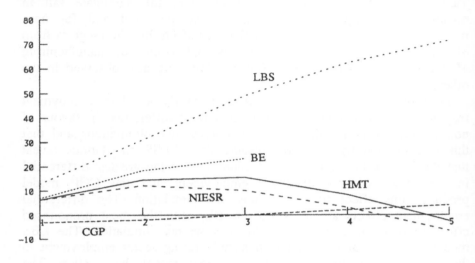

year

(b) effects on employment in non-manufacturing - differences from base run (thousands)

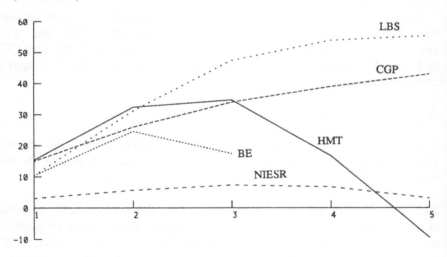

year

Figure 3.2   *Income tax simulation*

(a) effects on employment in manufacturing - differences from base run (thousands)

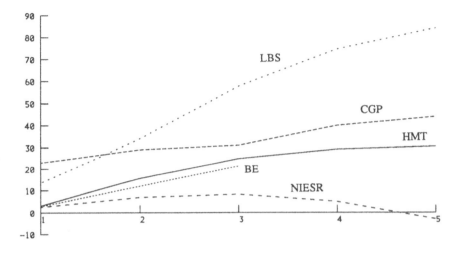

year

(b) effects on employment in non-manufacturing - differences from base run (thousands)

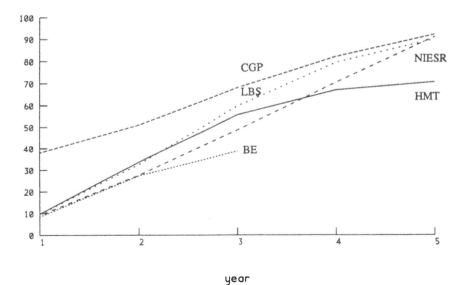

year

Figure 3.3 *VAT simulation*

(a) effects on employment in manufacturing - differences from base run (thousands)

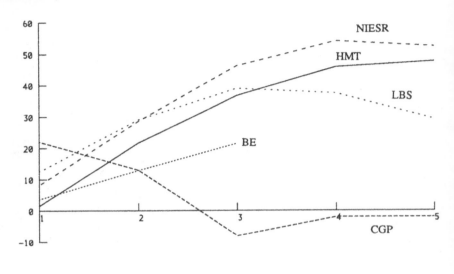

year

(b) effects on employment in non-manufacturing - differences from base run (thousands)

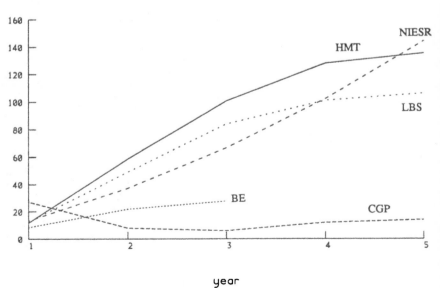

year

Figure 3.4   *Interest rate simulation*

(a) effects on employment in manufacturing - differences from base run (thousands)

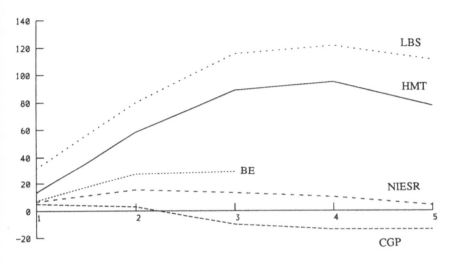

year

(b) effects on employment in non-manufacturing - differences from base run (thousands)

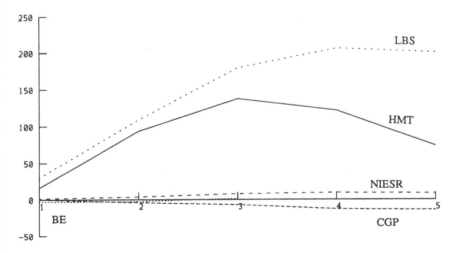

year

Figure 3.5   *Oil price simulation*

(a) effects on employment in manufacturing - differences from base run (thousands)

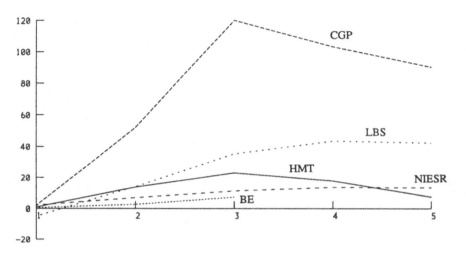

year

(b) effects on employment in non-manufacturing - differences from base run (thousands)

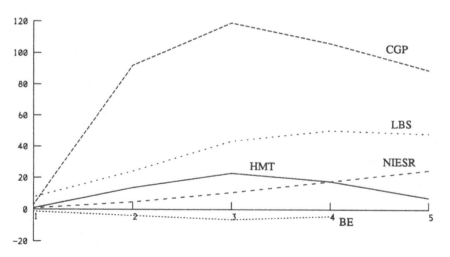

year

which boosts net trade. There is greater diversity among the models in terms of the effects on employment in non-manufacturing. The LBS still generates the largest employment response, but this is almost matched by the CGP. In contrast, the NIESR estimate is much smaller than that for the other models. In the other models increases in consumption, stockbuilding and investment are the main expansionary factors, but only consumption is a major influence for the CGP model. Clear signs of crowding out can be seen from the HMT model and this affects all the main domestic expenditure elements.

The income tax simulation. In the income tax simulation the greatest impact on manufacturing employment once again appears in the LBS model, with the weakest effect yet again appearing for NIESR. The CGP, HMT and BE results are all fairly similar. There is quite close association between the employment responses in non-manufacturing in the different models. After five years the effects in the CGP, LBS and NIESR models almost exactly coincide. The main expenditure items underlying the increase in GDP are similar to those observed in the government expenditure simulation. In particular, the rise in domestic demand in the CGP model is almost entirely owing to higher consumption as the level of prices falls due to weaker wage pressure associated with higher take-home pay. This effect otherwise appears only in the HMT model, but in this case there is also a strong increase in investment. We note here that the CGP model generates a higher employment response in both sectors than does HMT, despite a weaker output effect.

The reduction in VAT rates. In the case of the reduction in the rate of VAT, the BE and CGP models generate a lower aggregate employment response than do the other models and this is reflected in sectoral output effects. In the case of CGP this weak overall response arises from an appreciation of the exchange rate with its consequences for net trade. Consumption expenditure increases but not by enough to offset the net trade effect and the induced fall in investment. The net trade implications are a fall in manufacturing output and employment with a smaller decline in output for non-manufacturing. In the other models the exchange rate either depreciates or is unaffected so that the deterioration in net trade does not occur to the same degree. In addition, there is a rise in fixed investment and stockbuilding so that the effects on output in both manufacturing and non-manufacturing are much larger than for CGP. The employment effects on manufacturing and non-manufacturing are similar for the LBS, NIESR and HMT models.

The interest rate simulation. In the interest rate simulation the model responses vary from negligible (NIESR, BE and CGP) to substantial (LBS and HMT). In the LBS model aggregate output rises sharply in the short run as the exchange rate depreciates in order to maintain uncovered interest parity. The primary expenditure contributions to higher growth come from consumption, and particularly from fixed investment and stockbuilding as a direct response to lower interest rates. Similar effects are observed for HMT although the exchange rate reaction is less immediate. In the other models the exchange rate either falls very slightly (NIESR and BE) or appreciates (CGP). Given that direct interest rate effects are also quite weak in these models there is little change in aggregate output and employment, and hence in its sectoral components.

In the LBS model output in manufacturing rises by more than in non-manufacturing and the reverse holds for HMT, despite the very similar effects on the composition of expenditure. This is a clear case where the disaggregation process itself generates different sectoral effects despite the similar methodological approach whereby disaggregation proceeds from an allocation of final expenditure changes. In addition there are sectoral differences in the output-employment responses under this simulation. In the LBS model non-manufacturing employment increases by more than does output in this sector, but the reverse holds for HMT.

The effects of reducing the world oil price. The final simulation describes the effect of reducing the world oil price by 10 per cent while leaving all other indicators of world activity and prices unchanged. In general, output is increased and unemployment lowered as a compensation. However, the relative output effects across the models differ according to the reaction of the exchange rate. In the CGP model there is a very sharp decline (due to a fall in the value of oil reserves) and this generates a relatively high aggregate output response. The exchange rate also falls in the LBS and HMT models although not so dramatically, but in contrast there is little reaction by the exchange rate in the BE and NIESR models, and hence little impact on output. The effects on employment in manufacturing for CGP are far greater than for the other models owing to the boost to net trade, and the dominance of the aggregate output effect for this model is also reflected in the results for non-manufacturing.

Conclusions. Although the methods of disaggregation adopted are similar for many of the other models, the simulation responses in terms of manufacturing and non-manufacturing output and employment differ quite substantially. A key element in these differences is the behaviour of the exchange rate and its effect on net trade. Where the simulations generate a depreciating exchange rate this tends to favour output of manufacturing relative to that of non-manufacturing. Where an exchange-rate effect is absent the models tend to produce a balanced change in output in both sectors, with the exception of the income tax and VAT simulations which tend to be more favourable to non-manufacturing on account of the bias in expenditure change towards consumption. Employment implications follow in general from those of output, although there are one or two major exceptions to this (e.g. HMT for interest rates, NIESR for income tax).

3.4 Applicability of the models to policy questions

Despite the difficulties in using existing macro-models to test hypotheses concerning the Dutch disease (see Chapter 5 of Wallis (ed.), 1985), it does appear, at least, that the impact of alternative shocks on the manufacturing sector is dependent on the response of the real exchange rate. However, movements in this variable can be initiated by changes in monetary and fiscal policy, as well as by structural factors such as the extraction of new oil reserves. This implies that the development of the manufacturing sector is not entirely dependent on structural features of the economy. Whether policy measures should be addressed to reversing the decline of the manufacturing sector is beyond the scope of this chapter. What is clear is that substantial policy initiatives are required in order to achieve any noticeable turn-round in the prospects for this sector. The scale of response in the simulations described here suggests only a limited effect on relative sectoral outputs.

In the quarterly models this weak effect reflects the limited nature of the sectoral modelling. The use of fixed weights together with varying aggregate expenditure and the choice of weights itself embed, within the model, expenditure contributions relatively unfavourable to manufacturing. Since most of the quarterly models use very aggregate expenditure components of GDP (ignoring in several cases the richer disaggregated information on expenditure calculated by the model) the principal means by which manufacturing output (and employment) can be stimulated is by a trade-led expansion. Although there may be some validity in this implication its importance may be overstated by the modelling process. For example, possible counter-examples may be provided by the CGP model, although not by the simulation examples shown earlier. These would involve policy measures which may be disaggregated in themselves and this raises the general question of the potential use of the macro-models for policy questions. In the quarterly models policy instruments are actually relatively limited and are in general very aggregate. They mainly refer to fiscal policy and where disaggregation occurs it is usually in relation to the structure of government spending and taxation.

In contrast, the CGP model is better designed to answer policy questions with either new or more targeted policy measures than with standard fiscal operations. In this sense many of the models are inadequate to answer questions about the structure of the economy and its relation to policy since one might argue that it is implausible to expect aggregate policy measures to have marked sectoral effects. Even if this is not the case there is an even stronger argument for doubting the relevance of the non-CGP models to structural issues. One might argue that any plausible industrial policy should not be aimed at manufacturing as a whole, but at the elements of manufacturing which have the greatest potential. If structural analysis is to be based on a more 'micro' or case-study approach, then it is apparent that only the CGP model has anything worth offering in this respect.

4

MANUFACTURING AND SERVICES: SOME INTERNATIONAL COMPARISONS

*John Barber**

4.1 Introduction

The decline in the GDP share of manufacturing has in recent years been debated at great length by economic commentators. However, anyone trying to follow the debate may be forgiven for being confused. Some commentators take the view that the decline in manufacturing typifies all that is wrong with the British economy. Others imply that there is something inevitable and possibly even progressive about a declining share of manufacturing in GDP. The complexity of the issues involved owes much to the fact that the situation facing UK manufacturing industry is the product both of secular trends and the build-up of North Sea oil production since the late 1970s. The recent fall in world oil prices has merely served to focus more attention on what the effects of a fall in the real value of North Sea oil production might be. This paper looks at the decline in the share of manufacturing in UK GDP since the early 1960s and tries to set this decline in the context of what has happened in other countries. It then uses this comparison as a basis for discussing the reasons why the shift away from manufacturing may have occurred.

* The views expressed in this paper are those of the author who is writing in a personal capacity, not as a representative of the DTI. However the author is greatly indebted to a number of his colleagues who helped in the drafting of this paper, in particular Stephen Johnston, Stephen Aldridge and Vivien Booth.

4.2 The data

The comparison in the following tables is couched, wherever possible, in terms of three periods:

a) 1960-73, a period in which rapid and sustained growth was experienced in all industrialised nations;
b) 1973-78, the period, roughly speaking, from the cyclical peak prior to the first oil shock to the cyclical peak prior to the 1978-80 oil price shock;
c) 1978-84 the period since the second oil price shock. In a number of cases, especially for international comparisons, data availability dictates that an earlier terminal year is used.

Where international comparisons are made, figures for the UK are as quoted by the international source. These sometimes diverge from domestically produced estimates. For example, the OECD estimate of manufacturing share of GDP in the UK is different from the CSO estimate largely because the former expresses GDP at market prices rather than at factor cost.

4.3 The structure of UK GDP

Table 4.1 shows movements in the importance of major sectors of the UK economy since 1960 as measured by shares in current price GDP. Such an analysis is useful if only to remind us that manufacturing and services are not the only constituents of GDP and to show the impact of oil. The main features are as follows:

a) the share of manufacturing declined from 36.5 per cent in 1960 to 25.1 per cent in 1985;
b) the share of agriculture declined steadily throughout the period. By 1985 it accounted for only 1.8 per cent of UK GDP;
c) The energy sector, which doubled its share of GDP between 1960 and 1984, showed strong growth before and after the emergence of North Sea oil. The rise in the share of energy in current price GDP during the mid 1970s was the result of higher real oil prices combined with low (at least in the short term) elasticities for the demand for and supply of oil and other forms of energy;

d) the construction sector increased in importance during the 1960s but declined in importance after 1973;

e) the service sector's share of current price GDP has risen steadily since 1960.

Table 4.1   *UK: sectoral shares in current price GDP*

	1960[a,b]	1973[b]	1978	1984	1985
Agriculture, forestry and fishing	4.0	3.0	2.4	2.1	1.8
Energy and water supply	5.7[c]	4.6	7.3	11.0	11.2
Manufacturing	36.5	31.7	29.6	24.8	25.1
Construction	6.0	7.6	6.3	6.2	6.1
Services	47.7	57.2	58.4	60.7	61.3
Adjustment for financial services	-	(4.0)	(3.9)	(4.9)	(5.5)

Notes: [a] 1968 SIC.
   [b] Subject to minor revisions.
   [c] Mining and quarrying, gas, electricity and water.
Source: CSO *UK National Accounts*, various issues.

Care must be taken when interpreting the share of sectors because of the statistical adjustment for financial services. The contribution of the financial services sector to GDP is calculated inclusive of net receipts of interest. These receipts represent, at least in part, payments by firms, individuals and government for services rendered by financial institutions. However, insufficient information is available to determine the exact allocation of these receipts between the company sector, the personal sector and government, still less to attempt a sectoral breakdown within the company sector. If the correct allocation were known, the value added of the relevant sectors could be reduced accordingly (and any remainder attributed to final consumers' purchases of financial services). Instead, net interest receipts are bundled together under the heading 'adjustment for financial services'. Given the size of the adjustment the computed shares of the various sectors in GDP cannot be regarded as too precise. This said, it is unlikely that any of the broad trends exhibited in Table 4.1 will have been significantly affected by the way the adjustment is treated.

4.4 International comparisons

The shares of manufacturing and services

Turning now to developments in other countries, Table 4.2 shows trends in the shares of manufacturing and services in GDP at current prices for the UK, USA, Japan and the European OECD nations as a whole.

Table 4.2 *Current price value added in manufacturing as a percentage of GDP*

	UK		OECD-Europe[a]		USA		Japan	
	M	S	M	S	M	S	M	S
1960	32.1	53.8	31.4	48.1	28.6	57.7	33.9	42.9
1973	28.5	58.0	29.8	53.8	24.9	62.0	35.2	47.7
1978	26.5	60.0	27.6	56.9	24.4	62.9	29.6	53.7
1984	22.0	61.8	25.3	60.3	21.1[b]	66.3[b]	29.8	56.0

Notes: [a] OECD-Europe includes the UK.
        [b] 1983 (1984 not available).
Source: OECD, *Historical Statistics*, 1986 edition.

The share of manufacturing in current price value added fell steadily throughout the whole period 1960-84 in the UK, USA and OECD-Europe. In Japan, the share of manufacturing fluctuated, though the trend appears to be a downward one. In the period up to 1978 the decline in the share of manufacturing in current price GDP experienced by the UK was not significantly faster than that of the other countries. After 1978, the share of manufacturing does seem to have fallen more quickly in the UK. It must be remembered, however, that the increasing value of North Sea oil production after 1978 would have, simply as a matter of arithmetic, depressed the shares of GDP of all other UK sectors including manufacturing and services. The share of GDP devoted to services rose steadily in all countries throughout the period.

Changes in shares in current price GDP result from relative movements in both real output growth and in prices. Changes in sectoral shares in constant price GDP reflect divergent movements in real output only. Table 4.3 compares these two measures of the changing importance of different sectors. It shows that part of the explanation for the decline in manufacturing share in GDP lies in a decline in the prices of manufactures relative to other constituents of GDP as a whole. In the UK, USA and West Germany constant price shares of manufacturing in GDP fell less sharply than the current price shares between 1973 and 1983, most of the divergence occurring in the second half of the period. In Japan the steady fall in current price share of manufacturing between 1973 and 1983 is contrasted by the sharp rise in the constant price share over the same period.

Table 4.3   *Shares of manufacturing in GDP: a comparison of constant^a and current price data*

| | UK | | USA | | JAPAN | | WEST GERMANY | |
	Constant	Current	Constant	Current	Constant	Current	Constant^b	Current
1973	31.8	28.5	26.0	24.9	32.6	35.2	37.9	36.3
1978	29.3	26.5	24.9	24.4	33.8	29.6	36.4	34.1
1983	25.0	21.2	23.4	21.1	41.1	29.1	34.7	31.4

Notes: ^{a} All constant price data at factor cost. Base years: UK, 1980; USA, 1975; Japan, 1975; West Germany, 1976.
^{b} Includes Quarrying and Steel construction.
Source: Current price data, OECD *Historical Statistics*. Constant price data, *United Kingdom National Accounts* and OECD *National Accounts*.

Output and productivity

Another way of viewing the situation is to examine changes in output and productivity of manufacturing and services over time. This is done in Table 4.4. The table illustrates the point about changing relative prices. During the period 1960-73 the volume of UK manufacturing and services output grew at the same rate, thus implying that the fall in manufacturing's share in current price GDP relative to that of services was entirely due to the increased relative price of services. The picture is similar for the other countries shown.

During the years 1973-78, however, manufacturing output grew more slowly than that of services in all four countries shown. Accordingly, output changes are much more important in explaining the rise of services relative to manufacturing than in the period 1960-73. During

Table 4.4   *Output and productivity (annual average percentage change)*

		Manufacturing			Services	
		Output	Productivity	Employment[a]	Output	Productivity	Employment[a]
UK	1960-73	3.0	3.6	(-0.6)	3.0	1.7	(1.3)
	1973-78	-0.8	0.7	(-1.5)	1.4	0.3	(1.1)
	1978-84	-1.4	3.3	(-4.7)	1.8	0.8	(1.0)
OECD-[b]	1960-73	5.8	5.1	(0.7)	4.6	2.7	(1.9)
Europe	1973-78	1.6	2.5	(-0.9)	3.0	1.3	(1.7)
	1978-84	0.9	3.0	(-2.1)	2.1	0.6	(1.5)
USA	1960-73	4.9	3.4	(1.5)	4.1	1.3	(2.8)
	1973-78	1.7	1.0	(0.7)	3.5	0.3	(3.2)
	1978-84[c]	-0.2	1.6	(-1.8)	1.8	-0.1	(1.9)
Japan	1960-73	13.2	9.5	(3.7)	9.2	6.3	(2.9)
	1973-78	3.0	4.8	(-1.8)	4.3	2.1	(2.2)
	1978-84	7.5	6.2	(1.3)	3.6	1.5	(2.1)

Notes: [a] Changes in employment are implied only.
         [b] OECD-Europe includes the UK.
         [c] 1978-1983.
Source: OECD *Historical Statistics*.

the final period examined, only in Japan did manufacturing output rise faster than that of services. In the UK and USA manufacturing output actually fell. In all countries services showed modest output growth.

The main factor in the rising relative price of services is the growth in labour productivity of services compared to that of manufacturing. The measured growth in the labour productivity of services[1] (growth in value added per person employed) is inferior to that of manufacturing in every country/region in each time period. To the extent that gains in productivity are passed onto consumers, that wages rise at a similar rate in the two sectors, and that services are at least as labour intensive as manufacturing, this clearly implies a rise in the relative price of services.

---

[1]   See Section 4.7 below for a discussion of the problems in measuring service sector productivity.

Table 4.4 also brings out some important features of the UK's performance compared with its competitors. Firstly, the performance of UK services in terms of productivity growth is, if anything, worse relative to that of OECD-Europe or Japan than is that of UK manufacturing. However the UK service sector's productivity performance relative to that of the USA service sector was much better than that of UK manufacturing relative to its USA counterpart. Secondly, all four countries show the same pattern of declining growth rates in output of both manufacturing and services with only two exceptions. The exceptions are the acceleration in the rate of growth of Japanese manufacturing output and of UK service output, both after 1978. This last instance apart, however, UK growth rates have been invariably below those of the other three. Thirdly, the Japanese performance is exceptional in that it achieved massive growth in output and productivity in both manufacturing and services.

Employment

The changes in employment implied by the data in Table 4.4 are reflected in Table 4.5 which shows that the share of manufacturing in total civilian employment fell markedly in the UK from the relatively high figure of 1960. Elsewhere, it has fallen more modestly and in Japan it is only in the 1970s that a decline occurred. Although the fall since 1960 in the UK has been relatively large, manufacturing still accounted for a greater proportion of civilian employment in 1984 than in many competitor countries.

Table 4.5 *Employment in manufacturing as a percentage of civilian employment*

	UK	OECD-Europe[a]	USA	Japan
1960	38.4	27.3	26.4	21.3
1973	34.7	28.0	24.8	27.4
1978	32.0	26.5	22.7	24.5
1984	26.0	23.5	20.0	24.9

Note: [a] OECD-Europe includes the UK.
Source: OECD *Historical Statistics*.

4.5 Trends within manufacturing

Table 4.6 shows the five sectors of manufacturing whose share of total manufacturing GDP fell most sharply during the periods 1963-72 and 1973-84. Those sectors which declined in relative importance during 1973-84 are predominantly those which had declined prior to 1973. Similarly, many of those sectors which increased their share of manufacturing GDP in the later period were already growing in importance before 1973 (see Table 4.7).

Table 4.6 *UK manufacturing sectors in relative decline*

	1963-72[a]		Change 1963-72		1973-84[b]		Change 1973-84
	Share in manufacturing GDP (current prices)				Share in manufacturing GDP (current prices)		
	1963	1972			1973	1984	
Metal manufacturing	8.2	6.5	-1.7	Motor vehicles and parts	8.0	5.3	-2.7
Textiles	7.4	5.9	-1.5	Metal manufacturing	5.7	3.5	-2.2
Vehicles	11.2	10.0	-1.2	Textiles	5.1	3.0	-2.1
Clothing and footwear	3.6	3.1	-0.5	Metal goods (n.e.s.)	6.3	5.4	-0.9
Leather, leather goods and fur	0.5	0.4	-0.1	Clothing and footwear	4.2	3.5	-0.7

Notes: [a] 1968 SIC.
        [b] 1980 SIC.
Source: *UK National Accounts*, various editions.

Tables 4.8 and 4.9 compare the structural changes within UK manufacturing with those occurring in other OECD countries over the period 1973-82. In Table 4.8 changes in shares of manufacturing value added are measured at the broad two-digit ISIC level of aggregation (except for group 38, fabricated metal products). From the table it would appear that, at this level, structural change within manufacturing has followed a broadly similar pattern in all four countries. Sectors such as

Table 4.7   *UK sectors increasing their share in total manufacturing*

	1963-72[a] Share in manufacturing GDP (current prices)		Change 1963-72		1973-84[b] Share in manufacturing GDP (current prices)		Change 1973-84
	1963	1972			1973	1984	
Paper, printing and publishing	7.8	9.0	+1.2	Electrical & instrument engineering	11.1	14.3	+3.2
Food, drink and tobacco	11.2	12.3	+1.1	Chemicals & man-made fibres	8.6	10.9	+2.3
Other manufacturing	3.4	4.2	+0.8	Paper, printing & publishing	8.4	9.9	+1.5
Electrical and instrument engineering	10.5	11.1	+0.6	Food, drink & tobacco	12.4	13.8	+1.4
Timber, furniture etc.	2.9	3.3	+0.4	Other transport equipment	4.2	5.1	+0.9

Notes: [a] 1968 SIC.
         [b] 1980 SIC.
Source: *UK National Accounts*, various editions.

textiles, apparel and leather, wood products, and metal industries suffered a relative decline in all countries while others such as chemical products and machinery expanded their share.

Table 4.9 looks at the situation at a more disaggregated level. Sectors are classified as declining, static or growing at the three-digit ISIC level according to overall trends in output volumes in the four countries as a whole.[2] The shares of these three-digit industries are then added together to form declining, static and growing sectors. Although the results using this method are very sensitive to the definition of marginal industries (in terms of whether they are growing or static etc.) and to the level of aggregation, structural change in the UK would appear to have been at least as rapid as in the USA, West Germany, and Japan. The move into growth sectors in the UK has if anything been more marked than abroad.

---

2   See Table 4.9 fn (a) for a more detailed explanation.

Table 4.8 *Changes in industrial structure, 1973-82 (current price shares in manufacturing value added ^{a})*

ISIC Group	United Kingdom			USA			West Germany			Japan		
	1973 share	1982 share	change	1973 share	1981 share	change	1973 share	1982 share	change	1973 share	1982 share	change
31 Food, beverages and tobacco	12.9	15.0	+2.1	10.5	10.5	-	13.1	10.4	-2.7	8.1^c	9.4^c	+1.3
32 Textiles, apparel and leather	8.8	6.0	-2.8	7.6	6.1	-1.5	6.8	4.6	-2.2	8.8	6.1	-2.7
33 Wood products and furniture	3.6	3.1	-0.5	3.7	2.8	-0.9	4.2	2.8	-1.4	4.6	3.1	-1.5
34 Paper, paper products and printing	8.2	9.5	+1.3	9.2	9.8	+0.6	4.4	4.0	-0.4	7.2	7.9	+0.7
35 Chemical products	14.4	15.7	+1.3	14.6	16.1	+1.5	17.4^b	19.9^b	+2.5	14.4	14.8	+0.4
36 Non-metallic mineral products	4.5	4.7	+0.2	3.5	3.0	-0.5	5.3	3.8	-1.5	5.1	4.8	-0.3
37 Basic metal industries	7.5	4.6	-2.9	6.7	5.7	-1.0	8.4	6.1	-2.3	10.4	8.4	-2.0
38 Fabricated metal products	39.1	40.6	+1.5	42.7	44.6	+1.9	39.6	47.7	+8.1	39.8	43.9	+4.1
of which:												
381 Metal products	7.0	6.4	-0.6	6.8	6.7	-0.1	5.6	6.8	+1.2	6.9	6.4	-0.5
382 Machinery n.e.s.	11.1	12.2	+1.1	11.5	13.8	+2.3	12.2	14.6	+2.4	11.2	12.3	+1.1
383 Electrical machinery	8.2	9.8	+1.6	8.9	9.8	+0.9	10.6	12.3	+1.7	10.6	13.2	+2.6
384 Transport equipment	11.1	10.7	-0.4	12.5	10.5	-2.0	9.4	12.4	+3.0	9.7	10.3	+0.6
385 Professional goods	1.7	1.5	-0.2	3.0	3.8	+0.8	1.8	1.6	-0.2	1.4	1.7	+0.3
39 Other manufacturing n.e.s.	1.1	0.9	-0.2	1.7	1.6	-0.1	0.7	0.6	-0.1	1.5	1.5	-

Notes: ^{a} Total percentage shares may not add to 100 because of rounding.

^{b} Excludes petroleum & coal products.

^{c} Excludes tobacco.

Sources: UN *Yearbook of Industrial Statistics*; OECD *Industrial Structure Statistics*.

Table 4.9   *Structural change, 1973-82*

	Share of manufacturing value added in declining, static and growing sectors[a]		
	1973	1982[b]	Change
UK:			
declining	32.6	26.6	-6.0
static	24.5	22.6	-1.9
growing	43.0	50.9	+7.9
USA:			
declining	30.7	28.1	-2.6
static	24.5	22.4	-2.1
growing	45.0	49.7	+4.7
West Germany:			
declining[c]	35.2	28.5	-6.7
static	22.2	26.1	+3.9
growing	42.5	45.3	+2.8
Japan:			
declining	37.5	31.0	-6.5
static[d]	20.3	19.3	-1.0
growing	42.1	49.6	+7.5

Notes: [a] Sectors are defined as declining, static or growing according to average trends in indices of output for the period 1973-82 for the four countries as a whole. A declining sector is defined as one in which output grew significantly less than output in manufacturing as a whole in the majority of countries examined. A growing sector is one in which output grew significantly more than that of manufacturing as a whole in the majority of countries examined. All other sectors are defined as static.

Declining sectors	Static sectors	Growing sectors
321 Textiles	314 Tobacco	311/2 Food
322 Wearing apparel	341 Paper & products	313 Beverages
323 Leather & products	351 Industrial chemicals	342 Printing & publishing
324 Footwear	355 Rubber products	352 Other chemicals
331 Wood products	361 Pottery, china etc.	356 Plastic products
332 Furniture & fixtures	362 Glass & products	382 Machinery n.e.s.
353 Petroleum refineries	384 Transport equipment	383 Electrical machinery
354 Petroleum & coal products		
369 Non-metallic products n.e.s.		
371 Iron & steel		
372 Non-ferrous metals		
381 Metal products		
390 Other manufacturing		

[b] USA 1981.
[c] Excludes coal and petroleum products.
[d] Excludes tobacco.
Source: UN *Yearbook of Industrial Statistics*; OECD *Industrial Structure Statistics*.

Although, for the reasons stated above, it would not be wise to infer too much from the analysis on trends within manufacturing, it seems fair to say that structural change within UK manufacturing has not been in any way unusual when compared to the experience of our major competitors.

4.6 Factors affecting the decline of manufacturing relative to services in GDP

As shown above, the manufacturing sector as a share of GDP has declined in a number of other countries as well as the UK. That a similar change has occurred in these countries can be attributed to the operation of a number of factors which are common to many countries, such as differential price movements and income elasticities for manufacturing and services, and the effects of recession. The operation of such factors is illustrated below by reference to UK evidence. In addition, there are some other factors which have affected manufacturing which appear peculiar to the UK (and perhaps a few other countries) such as the quality of human capital and the consequences of the rising value of North Sea oil production.

4.7 Factors affecting all (or most) countries

Relative price effect

As explained in the previous section, in all countries/regions examined the rise in the price of services relative to manufacturing appears to have been a significant factor in depressing the current price share of manufacturing, particularly prior to 1973. One major cause of this price effect is the slower rate of growth in labour productivity in services compared to manufacturing. Unfortunately it is difficult to be categorical on this point because there are enormous difficulties in measuring the output and hence the productivity of the service sector. In most countries a mixture of methods is used to calculate service sector output. Four of the most common measures are:

a) deflated money value of output;
b) counting physical quantities of output;

c) deflating the wage bill;
d) counting the number of employees.

Clearly some of these measures may underestimate output changes and in cases where these are positive, productivity growth will be understated. In the case of the structure of (d), which is often used in measuring public services output (as well as the output of some private sector services), productivity change is zero by definition, though the assumption is sometimes made that productivity grows at the same rate as the economy as a whole in sectors whose output is measured in this way. The study by Smith (1972) of the period 1951-66 suggests that the average annual growth rate of output in services in the UK was proportionately understated by between 7 per cent to 11 per cent in official data. Even if the measurement of the quantity of service output presented no problems, difficulties in accounting for changes in the quality of service sector output would still give rise to unreliable productivity statistics.

The demand for manufacturing and services

Within the UK Treasury model, the index of the domestic demand for manufactures (derived from the CSO's *Commodity Flow Accounts*) shows that between 1970 and 1983 real domestic demand for manufactures grew more slowly than non-oil real private sector final expenditure; see Gleed's (1986) study of modelling imports of manufactures. However the same study also shows that the demand for manufactures shows a greater degree of cyclicality than non-oil total final expenditure and so comparisons are sensitive to time periods chosen.[3] However, Chapter 2 shows that the share of manufactures in UK domestic demand is projected to fall slowly over the period 1978-2000.

Many economists have suggested that a growing proportion of GDP will be accounted for by services because they have relatively high income elasticity of demand. A recent article (Bank of England, 1985b) produced cross-sectional data from the Family Expenditure Survey apparently supporting this proposition, i.e. at given relative prices, the share of total household expenditure spent on services tends to rise as

---

[3]   The series for the domestic demand for manufactures used by Gleed excludes food, drink and tobacco which tend to move in a less cyclical pattern than other components of manufacturing demand. However, the series for total demand for manufactures in the CSO Commodity Flow Account also appears to show a greater degree of cyclicality than demand in the economy as a whole.

total spending increases. However, the same article also contains evidence that for a given level of income, the proportion of expenditure on services (in constant prices) has fallen over time suggesting, perhaps, that the tendency for the relative price of services to rise exerts a depressing effect on consumers' demand for them. Of course, a relatively high income elasticity of demand is not in itself sufficient to cause a rise in the proportion of GDP accounted for by services, as there are a number of other factors at work. Gershuny and Miles (1983) noted the tendency for consumer services to be increasingly provided by a combination of manufactured consumer goods and 'self-service' labour input (for example, purchasing a washing machine rather than going to a launderette). This serves to illustrate that at the point of end use the distinction between manufacturing and services is not always clear cut and that the shares of services and manufacturing in final demand may be affected by the way in which the demand for a particular service is met.

Services as an input to manufacturing

The particular way in which producer services are supplied to manufacturing industry can have a significant influence on the measured shares of manufacturing and services in GDP. In September 1985 27.4 per cent of UK manufacturing employees were classified to administrative, clerical and technical occupations. Whiteman (1981) estimated that in 1971 only half of the employees in companies classified as manufacturing were in fact engaged in purely manufacturing occupations and some evidence suggests that in a number of manufacturing companies the proportion is even less. Although the proportion of employees classed as administrative, clerical and technical does vary with the business cycle, these results are enough to demonstrate how blurred the division between manufacturing and services can be.

There is also a considerable amount of anecdotal and other evidence that subcontracting of service functions from manufacturing has increased in recent years. In a recent NEDO study of changing work patterns (Atkinson and Neager, 1986) 70 per cent of companies sampled had increased their use of subcontractors. The vast majority of these had increased subcontracting of ancillary services. Another survey carried out for Manpower Ltd during 1985 showed that of companies in the production sector in their sample, 45 per cent had increased the volume of business carried out by subcontractors or the self-employed. This trend was expected to continue in the future. An Institute of Manpower study (Connor and Pearson, 1986) of information technology (IT) manpower, one of the fastest growing employment sectors, suggest that subcontracting of such staff is common, particularly among large electronics companies and industrial IT user companies. Another report by the IMS (Rajan and Pearson, eds, 1986) predicted that roughly half the jobs that may disappear from index of production industries between 1985 and 1990 (roughly 650,000, 450,000 of which would be in manufacturing) would reappear as subcontracted jobs in services. Finally, in a recent article by Ray (1986) an attempt is made to quantify the impact that the shift of service functions to organisations outside manufacturing has had on manufacturing output. Using certain assumptions, Ray estimated that manufacturing output could have been as much as 3.8 per cent higher in 1983, if all the increase in manufacturers' purchases of business, professional and leasing services since 1973 level had been performed in house rather than obtained from outside suppliers.

To the extent that subcontracting takes place (or even that there is a move towards siting services functions of manufacturing companies in separate establishments), there may be a statistical, as opposed to a real, shift from manufacturing to services, whose only significance is that it represents what firms see as a more efficient way of organising production.

Rising energy prices

Sharp rises (and falls) in the price of oil and other forms of energy can affect the demand for manufactures at both the microeconomic and macroeconomic levels. In this chapter the latter are taken to be subsumed in those of cyclical variations generally. Several different types of microeconomic effects resulting from higher energy prices can be identified. Some manufactured goods (e.g. petrochemicals, steel, cement) are much more energy intensive in their production than the general run of goods and services, so that the relative prices of these goods tends to rise when relative energy prices rise, which exerts a depressing influence on the demand for them. By contrast, rising energy prices may result in conservation measures by energy consumers which involve increased use of capital equipment or insulating materials, which, in turn, will increase the demand for those parts of manufacturing producing such goods. A sharp change in the price of oil will affect the demand for other energy sources, such as coal, nuclear power and renewables, whose production and/or consumption may involve greater use of manufactured capital equipment. Finally, sharp changes in energy prices can involve a significant transfer of purchasing power between producers and consumers of energy whose propensity to consume manufactures may be quite different. Identifying the impact on the share of manufactures in GDP of all these often very complex effects is very difficult, to say the least, but it should not automatically be assumed that this impact is necessarily trivial.

Recession

As noted above, the demand for manufactures tends to show a greater cyclicality than the other components of total demand in the economy. Table 4.10 shows the indices of constant price demand for the output of various sectors of the economy 1978-84. Construction apart, the domestic demand for manufactures fell further during the recent recession than did that of all other broad sectors of the economy and has subsequently staged a greater recovery. For this reason alone one might expect the share of GDP taken by manufacturing to fall in recessions and increase in upswings relative to its underlying trend.

Table 4.10 *The demand for manufactures and the recession*

Index of constant price domestic demand[a] for the output of various sectors of the UK economy (1980=100)

	1978	1979	1980	1981	1982	1983	1984
Whole economy	102.5	105.7	100	97.1	98.9	102.4	105.8
Manufacturing	108.4	112.1	100	95.8	97.4	104.0	107.7
Services[b]	97.5	102.1	100	99.9	102.7	106.5	112.1
Agriculture, forestry and fishing	98.7	98.2	100	98.7	105.8	103.0	106.7
Construction	106.2	106.7	100	90.2	92.5	96.6	99.3
Energy and water	104.2	107.2	100	93.2	92.6	92.6	89.6

Notes: [a] Output + imports - exports.
   [b] Services = distribution and repair, hotels and catering, transport, postal services and telecommunications and miscellaneous services.
Source: CSO *Commodity Flow Accounts.*

Newly-industrialising countries

It is arguable whether the rise of the newly-industrialising countries (NICs) has adversely affected manufacturing as a whole in developed countries. The Hayes Report (1979), which considered the case of the UK, concluded that the increases in imports of finished manufactures from NICs over the years prior to 1979 had been balanced by increases in exports to them, and that the impact of NICs' imports to the UK was roughly similar to that of other OECD countries. The sectors particularly affected by competition from NICs were mature industries, such as textiles, clothing and footwear. NICs therefore offer a partial explanation for some of the structural changes which are apparent in Table 4.7. The report warned, however, that other more technologically advanced sectors might in future become subject to increased competition from NICs. This would appear to have been borne out by, for example, the recent rise in the exports of integrated circuits from South Korea.

As indicated above, the growth in manufactured imports from NICs will have required some structural adjustment within the economies of developed countries (the growth of imports from Japan will have had a much greater impact on industrial structure in other developed countries). For the most part the shift in comparative advantage will be from one type of manufactures (often those that are labour intensive) to other manufacturing sectors. However, to the extent that the comparative advantage of the UK and other developed nations shifts towards services, it is likely that the share of services in GDP will rise relative to that of manufacturing in these countries.

4.8 Factors primarily affecting the UK

It is likely that the five factors discussed above will have had an impact on the shares of manufacturing and services in most major OECD countries. There are however some features of the UK economy which may have helped exaggerate the decline in the share of manufacturing since the 1960s, especially in recent years.

Secular decline

The UK's performance, usually typified by its performance in manufacturing, has been described as relatively weak since as far back as the Great Exhibition of 1851 and has certainly been so since 1960, the earliest year examined in this paper.

During the period of rapid growth, 1960-73, this did not manifest itself in a falling volume share of manufacturing in GDP. However, the growth of real manufacturing output in the UK only matched that of services during this period, while in other OECD countries manufacturing output grew more quickly than that of services. Since 1973, once again, the UK has failed to match the performance of its competitors, especially in manufacturing, but to a large extent in services as well. Enormous amounts have been written about the reasons for the UK's long-term relative decline and, although there is not room for a full discussion of the issues here, a number of factors are worth mentioning.

There is considerable evidence which suggests that it is not the level of investment in the UK as a whole, or in manufacturing in particular, which is the main problem. Gross domestic fixed capital formation as a proportion of GDP in the whole economy and in manufacturing has not been significantly lower in the UK than in other major OECD countries. Indeed, it has been higher than in some of them. Similarly, Prais (1986) found that Britain's total stock of machinery per employee does not differ greatly from that of other countries and its average age is less than in France, West Germany and the USA.

At least as important is the use actually made of new investment. Despite the problems in measuring capital productivity by use of incremental output to capital ratios, evidence based on this measure does indicate that, over the past two decades at least, capital investment in the UK has not been as productive as elsewhere.

Increasingly, the consensus which is emerging is that much of the problem lies in the quality of human capital. The National Institute study of manufacturers' productivity in the UK and West Germany (Daly et al., 1985) concludes that it is the lack of technical expertise and training, rather than a lack of modern machinery, that is the stumbling block. Two recent studies (MSC/NEDO 1984 and 1985) comparing training in the UK with its competitors tend to suggest that investment in human capital does not receive adequate attention in British companies. Allied to this is the evidence of the efficiency, or lack of it, with which the service functions in manufacturing, e.g. marketing, management, design, are performed in the UK. Such weaknesses might be expected to affect the service sector as well, and one indication that this is the case is given in the productivity figures in Table 4.4.

Hitherto, UK manufacturing has been more exposed to international competition than has the service sector. While about 30 per cent of manufactures are traded, the aggregate figure for services is thought to be less than 10 per cent (though there is a large degree of variation within the service sector). This means that weaknesses in UK manufacturing performance are much more likely to be translated into loss of market share than is the case with services. How far this translates into a reduced share of manufacturing in GDP depends on a number of complex economic interactions, but it does seem likely that the relative weaknesses in UK economic performance have to some extent contributed to the falling share of manufacturing in GDP. This view is supported by Table 4.4 which suggests that, in the past at least, a more successful economic performance generally is associated with a faster real growth of manufacturing output relative to that of services.

North Sea oil

The exploitation of North Sea oil clearly played a part in the more rapid decline of UK manufacturing after 1978. In 1979 the second oil price shock took place and this was the first year of significant North Sea oil production. Between 1977 and 1981 the real exchange rate appreciated by about 40 per cent. Although this rise was probably due to a combination of factors, a large part was due to North Sea oil and much has been written about how this has affected the UK economy (see e.g. Byatt *et al.*, 1982).

It can be argued that a considerable part of the North Sea oil effect was on industries which would have declined anyway or where structural adjustment had been delayed. These industries were typically mature ones, which were already facing severe competition, and where price competitiveness is especially important. The appreciation of the exchange rate was bound to affect these industries most severely. Tables 4.7-4.9 suggest that the pattern of structural changes in the UK after 1973 was not significantly different from that before 1973 and was not unlike that experienced abroad. Many of the industries which declined in the late 1970s and early 1980s will not necessarily be the industries which will expand as the oil runs out, or as the result of a lower real value of oil production. It is likely that all sectors of manufacturing will benefit from any depreciation in the real exchange rate which occurs as a result of the falling value of North Sea oil production, but there are too many other factors affecting the industrial structure to predict the precise sequence of events. In a period of rapid technological change the

one thing we can be sure about is that the future will be rather different
from the past.

4.9 Conclusion

The shift in the structure of GDP to one being increasingly dominated
by the service sector is not new and is not peculiar to the UK. Nor are
some of the structural changes which have been occurring within
manufacturing. A number of reasons, common to all major OECD
countries, have been put forward to explain these changes, some more
important than others, and some which have more to do with the way in
which we organise economic activity rather than with a shift in
economic resources. These changes should not in themselves be a cause
of concern. What should be of concern is that the UK should be
internationally competitive and be in a position to derive the maximum
economic advantage from the opportunities which arise in whatever
sectors. This will mean exploiting structural change, not resisting it. The
aim must be to exploit the opportunities that will arise in the future, not
to recreate the past.

5

THE EMPLOYMENT EFFECTS OF EXPANDING SERVICE INDUSTRIES

Ciaran Driver[*]

5.1 Introduction

This chapter investigates the linkages between various service industries in the UK economy and aggregate groups, in particular manufacturing.[1] It is not intended to determine any causal pattern or to propose any grouping as an 'engine of growth'. Those such as Cornwall (1977) who have attempted to use linkages in this way can be faulted for circular argument since the flows of inputs and outputs are indeed circular.[2] Nevertheless, it is of interest to look at the implications for employment of different patterns of output growth and an input-output framework is suited to this study.

The investigation proceeds by examining the effect on employment income of an autonomous increase in various industry outputs.[3] The approach involves a summation of the direct employment income generated and that accruing indirectly owing to backward linkages. No account is taken of any Keynesian multiplier effect or further changes in the pattern of output as factor incomes impinge on final demand; to do

---

[*] I am grateful to former colleagues in the Economics and Statistics Division of NEDO for assistance and comments on an earlier draft.

[1] Part of this chapter draws on the methods of Robertson *et al.* (1982), Chapter 5. That analysis, however, was carried out on the 1972 *Input-Output Tables* and was based, therefore, on the 1968 SIC.

[2] Cornwall is saved from the charge of complete circular argument by stressing the technological potential of manufacturing output. However, this ignores the outstanding contribution to productivity of some service sectors such as management education.

[3] Employment income is not, of course, the same as employment, and the relationship between the two may vary with output.

so would require the use of a full economic model.[4] It should also be noted that the effects measured are all *average*, not marginal. The assumptions of autonomous increase in individual industry demand is later placed in a more realistic context by considering different industry compositions of demand, specifically consumer expenditure, government expenditure, fixed investment and exports. The data source is the 1979 *Input-Output Tables* published by the UK Central Statistical Office.[5] Rather than manipulate the entire 100 industry square array given in the Tables, the matrix was compressed into a more compact array, giving flows between the primary sector, the manufacturing sector, construction, and each of the twelve service industries shown in Table 5.1.

5.2 Employment income per unit of industry final demand

The first column of Table 5.1 shows the direct and indirect effects on employment income arising from a unit increase in final demand for each industry or sector. A description of the analytical steps and the methodology used may be found in Annex 5A. The second column shows the corresponding profits figure. Value added equal to the sum of these entries is shown in the last column.[6]

The figures in brackets in Table 5.1 show the ratio of the total employment income or value added to that arising within the industry in question. Thus, the total employment income effect for manufacturing is 1.4 times that arising within manufacturing itself, as a result of a unit

---

4   It would also be possible to endogenise some of the final demand vectors, but non-linearity is more likely to be a problem here than for material and labour inputs.

5   It may be helpful to give some brief comments on the interpretation of the service entries in the *Input-Output Tables*. In the case of distribution and transport it should be noted that the gross output includes only the sum of the gross margins on handling the goods, plus the purchase of commodities directly related, e.g. fuel. The output of post and communication on the other hand includes output which is not, strictly speaking, service output - communications equipment. (This type of output constitutes nearly a fifth of the industry's final output.) The output of the 'owning' industry also had an unusual feature in that it includes imputed rents in its value added. In the case of 'other services', the industries concerned are highly heterogeneous and the figures provided must be regarded as highly approximate.

6   In Table 5.1, the case of railways is unique in that both employment income and value added are greater than 1. Normally this is not possible, as the proceeds of final output must be at least sufficient to cover total factor incomes. In the case of railways, however, net subsidies are a third of gross output, and this observation seems to account for the peculiarity noted in the figures. The subsidy to railways per unit of final output is nine times the next largest figure (that for coal extraction) and five times the largest figure for tax per unit of final output. It can, therefore, be safely considered as a unique case.

Table 5.1   *Total employment income effect of a unit increase in final output by industry*[a]

Industry	Employment income	Profits	Value added
(1-9) Agriculture, other primary, and utilities	0.33 (1.7)	0.42	0.75 (1.3)
(10-87) Manufacturing	0.51 (1.4)	0.19	0.70 (1.5)
88 Construction	0.51 (1.6)	0.30	0.82 (1.5)
89 Distribution and repairs	0.59 (1.4)	0.27	0.86 (1.4)
90 Hotels, catering and public houses etc.	0.54 (2.1)	0.26	0.80 (2.0)
91 Railways	1.02 (1.3)	0.19	1.21 (1.4)
92 Road and other inland transport	0.54 (1.4)	0.30	0.84 (1.4)
93 Sea transport	0.28 (1.9)	0.14	0.42 (1.8)
94 Air transport	0.34 (1.8)	0.28	0.62 (1.8)
95 Transport services	0.67 (1.3)	0.22	0.88 (1.4)
96 Postal services and telecommunications	0.61 (1.2)	0.27	0.88 (1.2)
97 Banking, finance, insurance, and business services	0.81 (1.3)	0.07	0.88 (1.4)
98 Owning and dealing in real estate	0.35 (3.2)	0.54	0.89 (1.6)
99 Other services	0.71 (1.1)	0.22	0.93 (1.1)
100 Public administration, domestic services and ownership of dwellings	0.68 (1.0)	0.32	1.0 (1.0)

Note: [a]Total includes direct and indirect. The figures in brackets are the ratio of total incomes to those arising in specific industries, as described in the text. The row numbers refer to the *Input-Output Tables*.

increase in manufacturing final output.[7]

Table 5.2 ranks the industries by employment income per unit of output and value added and the differences mainly reflect the different factor incomes accruing directly, as a result of differing factor mix. Table 5.2 also includes a ranking of industries in terms of total (direct and indirect) import content. The close correspondence between this ranking and that of the other two services reflects the dominating influence of import requirements per unit in the determination of employment income and value added per unit. The horizontal broken line in Table 5.2 separates out the services which have a distinctly low employment income per unit of output, as detailed in Table 5.1.

One important point to note in the treatment of services is that Public Administration (including health and education) is assumed to have no material inputs. Such inputs clearly do exist (e.g. school furniture) but they are assumed to constitute final expenditure by general government. This allows the output of public administration to be recorded as value added, or the sum of factor incomes generated, so that employment input per unit of output may be artificially high.

5.3 Interdependence of services and manufacturing

In view of the attention generally focused on the interdependence between service industries and manufacturing, it is instructive to consider the linkages between these categories in terms of employment income. A detailed tabular presentation of these linkages is contained in Annex 5B, but it is possible to highlight the main points of interest more simply. This is done in Tables 5.3, 5.4 and 5.5.

Table 5.3 shows the non-manufacturing industries where employment shows a significant response to manufacturing output and Table 5.4 the industries where a unit increase in their final demand generates the largest increases in manufacturing employment income. There is no reason why the two sets of industries should be similar: the first set shows those industries most dependent on manufacturing; the second set shows the dependence of manufacturing on other industries. Indeed, the occurrence of agriculture, transport and distribution in both sets of

---

[7]   The ratios shown are not, strictly speaking, multipliers in the sense used by Robertson *et al.* (1982). A multiplier shows the ratio of total employment income or value added as a proportion of the original change in these occasioned by the increase in final output. This original change in factor income in the expanded industry will generally be somewhat smaller than the total change caused in that industry alone. Consequently, the ratios shown in Table 5.1 of this book will generally be smaller than the associated 'multipliers'.

Table 5.2   *Some characteristics of UK industries*

Industries ranked by

	Total employment income per unit of final output	Total value added per unit of final output	Inverse of total import content per unit of final output[b]
1	Railways[a]	Railways[a]	Public admin.[b]
2	Banking	Public admin.	Other
3	Other	Other	Banking
4	Public admin.	Owning	Transport services
5	Transport services	Banking	Owning
6	Post	Transport services	Distribution
7	Distribution	Post	Road
8	Hotels	Distribution	Post
9	Road	Road	Rail
10	Construction	Construction	Hotels
11	Manufacturing	Hotels	Construction
12	Owning	Agriculture	Agriculture
13	Air	Manufacturing	Manufacturing
14	Agriculture	Air	Air
15	Sea	Sea	Sea

Notes: [a] See note 5 to this chapter.
   [b] The data on which these ranks are based were taken from Table J of the *Input-Output Tables*. Figures are not available for the import content of public administration separately from the input to other final expenditure. A low rank can be assumed and the first rank was chosen arbitrarily.

strong linkages is somewhat fortuitous in one sense, though it also throws some light on why manufacturing is often singled out as a uniquely important sector, having strong linkages both ways with these three larger sectors. This important characteristic of manufacturing is strengthened when the construction industry is considered, although construction does not feature in Table 5.3. This is largely because of the ways the input-output tables are designed, with investment shown as final output rather than as an input to industry. However, an increase in manufacturing will undoubtedly stimulate construction strongly and in return construction output stimulates manufacturing employment.

The case of construction serves as a warning not to use the input-output tables as a value-free way of identifying the overall importance

Table 5.3   *Employment income by industry arising from a unit increase in final output of manufacturing*

Manufacturing	Agriculture etc.	Distribution	All transport and transport services	Other	Banking	Remainder	Total services
0.368	0.026	0.032	0.022	0.038	0.016	0.011	0.119

Table 5.4   *Employment income in manufacturing arising from a unit increase in final output of selected industries*

Railways	Construction	Hotels	Transport services	Agriculture etc.	Owning[a]	Distribution
0.133	0.105	0.098	0.071	0.059	0.055	0.053

Note: [a] The occurrence of 'owning etc.' in this group may be thought surprising. A large input to 'owning' from construction is being translated into indirect input from manufacturing. This may involve aggregation errors, however if the construction input is mostly in the form of repairs, decorating etc.

of any sectoral group in the economy. Public services for instance may have strong input linkages from the rest of the economy but these entries are shown as zero and are assumed to be consumed directly by general government. Similarly public sector output may constitute important inputs for the rest of the economy (e.g. in the case of education); but here again, like physical investment, the output is allocated to final demand and not shown as an input as it would be if the circular flows were fully represented.

Turning to the non-overlapping sets of industries in Tables 5.3 and 5.4, 'other services' and 'banking etc.' feature as industries which are strongly stimulated by increases in manufacturing.[8] This is not, of course, the same as defining them to be producer rather than consumer industries since an industry may respond relatively strongly to

8   The 'other services' category includes cleaning services, laundries, driving schools, private health and education, film, art, hairdressing, waste disposal, research and development, and various other activities. The majority of its output does not constitute 'consumer' services, however.

manufacturing, in the sense of employment generated per unit of manufacturing output, and nevertheless feed only a small percentage of *its own* output into manufacturing.[9] Further details on these forward linkages is given in Annex 5C.

Looking at the opposite type of linkage, the industries 'hotels etc.' and 'owning' give rise to a significant input from manufacturing.[10] Figures calculated from Annex 5B show that a unit increase in final output in hotels etc. and in owning etc. leads to employment income in manufacturing which is respectively 38 per cent and 47 per cent that of employment income generated in the industry concerned.

Table 5.5 brings together the information from previous tables. The industries are shown in order of rank of employment income per unit of output with the table split for convenience into top and bottom halves. The rankings for own employment income are shown in column (2). The corresponding ranks for input linkages from manufacturing and output linkages to manufacturing are also shown in the table.

The high correlation between the first two columns is evident, with the same industries occupying the first half of the table in each column. This indicates a close correspondence between direct and total employment income generation. Column (3) shows that the top seven employment income industries are associated with high-ranking industries in terms of linkages from manufacturing output to services. (The mean rank is 5 compared with a mean rank of 8 in the bottom half of column (3).) By contrast, column (4) shows no evident association between employment income rank and the rank of linkage from service output to manufacturing.

In view of the close correspondence between direct and indirect employment income figures, the association noted above between these variables and the extent of linkage from manufacturing output to services must be of a non-causal kind. In other words, the high total employment generated per unit of output is not due to indirect effects caused by the linkage with manufacturing. However, this does not affect the conclusion that, for whatever reason, high employment income service industries are those which respond strongly to manufacturing output, i.e. those where employment income generated per unit of

---

9   Indeed the industries used in the *Input-Output Tables* are too broad to allow for a sensible classification into 'producer' and 'consumer' industries. Almost all industries are an amalgam of both these categories. If the industries are classified on the basis of the ratio of intermediate plus capital formation flows to consumer expenditure flows, those closest to the consumer-oriented end are distribution, hotels, railways and owning. Producer-oriented industries are: construction, transport services, road, post and other. Air and sea industries are excluded from this analysis as they are heavily export oriented.

10   But see the note to Table 5.4.

Table 5.5   *Ranking of input and output linkages*

Industry	(1) Rank of total employment income per unit of each service industry's final output	(2) Rank of own employment income per unit of each service industry's final output	(3) Rank of employment income linkage from manufacturing output to services	(4) Rank of employment income linkage to manufacturing from services
Railways	1	1	8	1
Banking	2	3	4	9
Other	3	4	1	12
Public admin.[a]	4	2	-	-
Transport				
Services	5	5	6	4
Post	6	6	7	10
Distribution	7	7	3	7
Hotels	8	10	10	3
Road	8	8	5	8
Construction	10	9	9	2
Owning	11	14	10	6
Air	12	11	10	11
Agriculture	13	11	2	5
Sea	14	13	10	13

Note: [a] Ranks have not been assigned for the last two columns.

manufacturing final output is relatively high.

The other conclusion to emerge from this study of linkage is that service industries whose outputs generate a higher than average response from manufacturing are not more likely to generate a higher than average total employment income per unit of output. Indeed there seems to be no clear relationship either way between the employment income generated and the tendency to induce manufacturing production. It is possible that this conclusion could be changed were inputs of fixed investment to be taken into account. Information on this is only available for some broadly defined industries, but it does appear that in regard to the service industries, plant and machinery inputs are most significant (in relation to intermediate inputs) for post and telecommunications, financial and other services. Thus the inclusion of fixed investment could result in a positive correlation between 'labour intensity' and linkage from services output to manufacturing.

A question arises as to whether linkages with the rest of the economy and in particular with manufacturing are a desirable feature for service industries to possess. Economists will differ in their views on this, but the following considerations seem relevant. First, a low input from manufacturing is likely to be correlated with a high direct labour input with corresponding restricted scope for productivity improvements, except of the labour displacing type. In contrast to this, capital (and materials) saving technical progress allows for an immediate increase in factor incomes with only a diluted negative effect on factor incomes in the supplying industries. Care must be taken here not to underestimate the potential productivity improvements from non-material inputs such as increased organisation, or skills.

Second, employment in services (as distinct from employment income) is often thought to be more stable than in other industries. For some services this feature may be due to a low income elasticity, while for others it may be explained by cyclically flexible wages and hours. Despite this flexibility, and low income elasticities for certain services, employment in this sector will be particularly vulnerable to a severe squeeze on household income. This is due to the high proportion of services output that feeds into final domestic consumption (Annex 5C). Rothschild (1981) notes that while trade and services accounted for 77 per cent of all new private employment in the US from 1920 to 1929, many of these jobs were lost after October 1929. Service employment in the UK held up rather well during the early thirties, but this may reflect the comparatively mild squeeze on UK incomes.[11] The last point on the vulnerability of services may be of no more than historical interest and this feature will presumably lessen with growth in producer services and exported services.

It seems that there is little in the way of *a priori* argument to support the case for strong linkages with manufacturing. Nevertheless, it may be important for policy makers to know that manufacturing output generates a strong stimulus to services employment income, while the effect of services output on employment will be mediated by decisions on investment and consumers' expenditure. Of course there are also other considerations on the demand side which may compel the promotion of activity with high value added per head, and some manufacturing activities out-perform some services on this count.

---

[11] The response of employment in different service groups to changes in the level and distribution of household income is explored in Driver and Naisbitt (1987).

5.4 Employment income arising from different categories of final demand

In this section, the attention turns to the effect on total employment income of increasing by one unit the value of the bundle of final outputs that constitute each of the different major components of total final demand - consumer expenditure, general government final consumption, gross fixed capital formation (GFCF) and exports of goods and services. The composition of each bundle is assumed fixed at 1979 values, in the same way as the technological coefficients of the input-output table are also taken as fixed.

The effect on each of its major constituents of increasing total final demand by one unit is shown in Table 5.6. The effect is shown separately for employment income and value added. From this table it is apparent that, for both employment income and value added, capital formation and exports produce roughly the same effect as an increase in the total final demand category. General government expenditure and consumer expenditure result in substantially greater and lesser effects respectively. Employment income and value added are closely correlated in this table.

Table 5.6   *Effect on total employment income and value added of a unit increase in final demand, by category*

	Consumer exp.	General govt	GFCF	Exports	Total[a]
Employment income	0.41	0.61	0.46	0.48	0.46
Value added	0.61	0.88	0.68	0.69	0.68

Note: [a] Including physical increase in stocks.

It may be of interest to compare the above totals for employment income with the amounts accruing to various sectors and sectoral groups. This information is shown in Table 5.7. It is apparent that manufacturing and construction are most stimulated by a rise in capital formation, with exports also being important in the case of manufacturing. General government, not surprisingly, has its biggest effect on 'public services', while 'private services' are stimulated fairly evenly by the different categories of expenditure, with consumer

Table 5.7   *Effect on employment income by sectoral group arising from a unit increase in final demand, by category*

	Consumer exp	General govt	GFCF	Exports	Total
Agriculture etc.	0.02	0.01	0.02	0.04	0.03
Manufacturing	0.11	0.08	0.17	0.24	0.14
Construction	0.01	0.01	0.13	0.01	0.03
Public services[a]	0.09	0.41	0.02	0.02	0.11
Private services[b]	0.18	0.10	0.13	0.17	0.16
Total services	0.27	0.51	0.14	0.19	0.27
	(0.26)	(0.54)	(0.11)	(0.21)	(0.27)

Notes: [a] Rail, air, post and public administration.
        [b] All other services except construction.
        Figures in brackets are for 1972 as calculated by Robertson *et al.* (1982).

expenditure and exports having the greatest effect. The effect of exports on services employment income is examined more closely in the following section. Table 5.7 also contains the 1972 figures for total services, obtained by Robertson *et al.* (1982). While there has undoubtedly been a saving on total employment income per unit of manufacturing output, this does not appear to be the case for services, though comparisons between single years are difficult. It will be of interest to examine the corresponding figures for later input-output tables when they are published.

5.5 Employment income and exported services

It is frequently argued that the key to future employment generation in the case of advanced industrialised countries is the expansion of exported services. This is held to follow from the high proportion of the workforce employed in services and the high proportion of export earnings generated from services. Many services, however, are not and cannot be exported and it is not immediately apparent what proportion of total employment income is generated by service exports. In order to answer this question, the relevant data have been brought together in Table 5.8.

Total employment income in all services (except public administration) may be calculated from the input-output tables as

Table 5.8 *Employment income arising from exports*

Industry	Exports	Implied gross output[a]	Direct employment income from exports[b]	Total employment income from exports[c]	Ratio of direct employment income from exports to industry employment income
Construction	161	209.3	51.9	82.8	0.008
Distribution	2264	2363.6	960.6	1333.0	0.067
Hotels	988	990	255.2	534.5	0.121
Rail	127	127.4	97.5	129.9	0.083
Road	250	252.4	96.5	135.5	0.038
Sea	3216	3225	489.2	897.3	0.757
Air	1075	1129.4	208.8	362.3	0.471
Transport services	646	666.7	322.7	432.2	0.182
Post	202	209.4	100.6	122.6	0.034
Banking	2614	2776.8	1661.4	2114.7	0.184
Owning	82	83.5	9.5	28.8	0.024
Other	1448	1483.2	900.2	1023.7	0.102
Total			5154.1	7197.3	

Notes: [a] Total requirements per unit of final output (including intra-industry flows).

  [b] Previous column multiplied by employment income per unit of gross output.

  [c] Exports multiplied by total employment income per unit of final output, obtained from Annex B.

£50855m in 1979. Expressing the direct employment income arising from exports of services as a ratio of this total gives a figure of 10.1 per cent for the proportion of services employment income arising from exports.[12]

From the last column in Table 5.8, it may be seen that some industries have a notably higher proportion of export-oriented employment - sea, air, banking, transport services, with 'hotels' and 'other' slightly above average. These six industries together account for three-quarters of the total (direct and indirect) employment income generated from exported services. It should be noted that public administration is recorded as having no exports. Adding in employment income in public administration to the total service employment income denominator lowers the proportion of export-oriented direct employment

---

[12] Tourist revenue giving rise to employment income is included in the direct employment income from exports only in so far as it reflects tourist revenue on services.

income in services to 7 per cent.

The fourth column in Table 5.8 gives the total (direct and indirect) employment income arising from services wherever it accrues. For all service industries considered, the ratio of total to direct employment income (7197.3/5154.1) = 1.40. This ratio shows that the total employment income generated in the economy as a result of services exports is 40 per cent higher than the direct income accruing to services.

5.6 Conclusions

This chapter has attempted to lay the groundwork for a discussion of sectoral inter-relationships in the economy by showing how service industries respond to or induce changes in each other and in the aggregate groups (agriculture etc.) and manufacturing. The response to various categories of final demand has also been investigated.

The analysis has focused on employment income, and a number of conclusions in respect of this have emerged:

1) The rankings of total employment income per unit of final output and the corresponding direct employment income figures are close.
2) The rankings of total employment income per unit of final output and the corresponding value added figures are close.
3) The rankings of total employment income per unit of final output are highly and inversely correlated with rankings of total import content per unit of final output.
4) The strength of linkage from manufacturing output to services employment income is directly associated with a high total employment income per unit of the service industry's final output.
5) The strength of linkage from service industry output to manufacturing employment income does not seem to be associated with any pattern of total employment income per unit of the industry's final output; however, a positive relationship is discernible if fixed investment is considered as an input.
6) The greatest effect on employment income is achieved when general government expenditure is stimulated; the least effect when consumer expenditure is stimulated.
7) Private services employment income is stimulated fairly evenly by different categories of final expenditure, with consumer expenditure and exports having the greatest effect.
8) The direct employment income effect of exported services is

about 10 per cent of total service employment (excluding public administration). The total employment income generated is about 40 per cent greater than this.

Annex 5A Methodology

The basic input-output relationship is of the form:

$$x = Ax + f$$

where x is a vector of gross output, by industry including intra-industry flows, f is a vector of final demand by industry, and A is the technical co-efficient matrix whose typical element a_{ij} represents the value of the ith input needed to produce one unit of industry j output.

Solving the matrix equation for x, we obtain $(I - A)^{-1}f$, where I is the identity matrix. The inverse, known as the Leontief inverse, represents the total requirements per unit of final industrial output in terms of gross output. With all elements of f set equal to zero except for the jth element, $(I - A)^{-1}f$ represents the total (direct or indirect) gross output by industry needed to produce a unit of the jth industry final output. With f constituted so that it represents the proportions of final output (including imports, taxes etc.) in any final output constituent such as consumer expenditure, or exports, $(I - A)^{-1}f$ represents the total (direct or indirect) gross output by industry needed to produce a unit of that type of final demand in that given combination.

The basic input-output tables also contain data on employment income and value added by industry. These were expressed per unit of gross output (including intra-industry flows). Term these co-efficient vectors e and v respectively where the co-efficients are arranged in column vectors. e and v may be re-arranged like the identity matrix I to yield diagonal matrices $\hat{e}$ and $\hat{v}$. These diagonal matrices when post-multiplied by $(I - A)^{-1}f$ give the total (direct or indirect) employment income and value added respectively, by industry corresponding to any f, in particular to the definitions of f outlined above.

If it is desired to obtain the total (direct or indirect) employment income summed over all industries, wherever it accrues as a result of any f stimulus, it is only necessary to premultiply $(I - A)^{-1}f$ by $\acute{e}$ (or $\acute{v}$), (transposed vectors), rather than the corresponding diagonal $\hat{e}$ (or $\hat{v}$) matrices. This has the effect of collapsing the rows of the latter matrix product.

Annex 5B

Table 5.9   *Data on linkages between manufacturing and services in terms of employment income*

	(1) Employment income[a] by industry arising from a unit increase in final output of manufacturing	(2) Employment income[a] by industry arising from a unit increase in final output of each industry	(3) Employment income[a] in manufacturing arising from a unit increase in final output of each industry	(4) Total employment income[a] arising from a unit increase in final output of all industries
Manufacturing	0.368	0.368	0.368	0.512
Agriculture etc.	0.026	0.192	0.059	0.331
Construction	0.003	0.323	0.105	0.514
Distribution etc.	0.032	0.424	0.053	0.589
Hotels etc.	0.001	0.258	0.098	0.541
Rail	0.004	0.768	0.133	1.023
Road etc.	0.009	0.386	0.048	0.542
Sea	0.001	0.152	0.026	0.279
Air	0.001	0.194	0.033	0.337
Transport services	0.007	0.500	0.071	0.669
Post etc.	0.006	0.499	0.039	0.607
Banking etc.	0.016	0.636	0.046	0.809
Owning etc.	0.001	0.116	0.055	0.351
Other	0.038	0.622	0.028	0.707
Public admin.[b]	0.000	0.681	0.000	0.681
Total services				

Notes: [a] Employment income induced through factor incomes is not considered.
[b] Conventionally, public administration is recorded as consuming no material inputs.

Annex 5C

Table 5.10 *Percentage output feeding into other industries and final output*

		(0-9)	(10-87)	(88)	(89)	(90)	(91)	(92)	(93)
Agriculture etc.	(0-9)	22	30	0	3	1	0	1	0
Manufacturing	(10-87)	3	28	4	3	1	0	0	0
Construction	(88)	3	1	23	2	0	0	0	0
Distribution	(89)	3	18	3	3	2	0	1	0
Hotels etc.	(90)	1	2	1	1	0	0	0	0
Railways	(91)	5	32	2	1	0	0	0	0
Road etc.	(92)	2	28	4	26	3	0	0	0
Sea	(93)	3	8	3	1	1	0	0	0
Air	(94)	3	13	2	5	0	0	0	0
Transport service	(95)	7	30	0	14	1	0	0	10
Post etc.	(96)	1	11	1	8	1	0	1	0
Banking etc.	(97)	1	11	1	8	2	0	2	1
Owning etc.	(98)	1	15	1	23	2	0	1	0
Other	(99)	6	35	1	4	4	0	0	0
Public admin.	(100)	0	0	0	0	0	0	0	0

Notes: [a] Consumer expenditure; general government expenditure; gross fixed capital respectively.
[b] Totals may not add to 100 owing to rounding errors.
Source: CSO (1979) *Input-Output Tables.*

Table 5.10 *continued*

(94)	(95)	(96)	(97)	(98)	(99)	(100)	(C)[a]	(G)[a]	(I)[a]	(X)[a]	(T)[a]	Row total[b] (%)
1	0	0	0	0	0	0	19	3	2	15	41	100
0	0	0	1	0	1	0	19	5	8	24	57	100
0	0	0	1	2	0	0	11	5	50	1	67	100
0	0	0	0	0	1	0	56	2	4	6	69	100
0	0	0	0	0	0	0	75	7	0	12	94	100
0	0	3	0	0	0	0	39	8	1	8	57	100
0	0	0	0	0	0	0	26	2	4	4	36	100
0	0	0	0	0	0	0	6	1	2	76	84	100
0	0	2	1	0	0	0	21	2	1	45	69	100
2	3	0	8	2	1	0	1	20	18	2	1	100
0	1	3	23	1	5	0	23	8	8	3	42	100
0	1	1	5	1	3	0	23	11	12	17	64	100
0	3	1	3	1	2	0	37	9	0	2	48	100
0	1	1	4	1	2	0	22	8	0	10	40	100
0	0	0	0	0	0	0	34	66	0	0	100	100

formation; exports; total final expenditure (including physical increase in stocks),

6

THE STRUCTURE OF SERVICE EMPLOYMENT IN THE UK

*Paul Dunne**

6.1 Introduction

From manufacturing to services

The shift from manufacturing to service-industry employment has been a common characteristic of all advanced industrial countries and has been particularly marked in the UK. Public and private services have become increasingly important sources of employment as manufacturing has been hit by recession and has adopted labour-saving technologies in attempts to gain international competitiveness. It is clear that the future of the service sector will have an important influence on the future of employment in the UK, but there is controversy about what that future will be, a debate fuelled by inherent conceptual and measurement problems which make consistent analysis and discrimination between explanations very difficult.

Until recently it was generally accepted that a move to a 'service economy' was both acceptable and viable, and that a low productivity growth service sector could indeed provide employment for workers being shed by manufacturing industry. Some writers, such as Gershuny (1978), questioned the ability of the service sector to provide adequate future employment, arguing that personal services tend towards 'self service' as households use manufactured goods to internalise their production. Innovations in service demand can increase the demand for manufacturing and a growing proportion of output is likely to be in

*   I am grateful to Bob Rowthorn for comments.

intermediate services, less labour intensive and more open to labour shedding technical progress. Robertson *et al.* (1982) argued against this position, claiming that Gershuny overstated the 'self service' effects and underestimated the externalisation of some household services and other compensating gains in expanding sectors.

The nature of service employment

There is also a related debate on the nature of the growth in service employment. Gershuny (1985) argues that there is evidence for the EEC that growth in service employment is not service employment growth *per se* but a changing occupational structure in the industrial sector. Momigliano and Siniscalco (1982) used Italian data to argue that the growth of services reflects the growing integration of services into the industrial system and that they do in fact require growth in other sectors. Their findings imply that the growth in service output has not been the result of a growth in the production of services *per se* but an increase in the demand for services in other industries. If this is the case, then the level of manufacturing required to sustain the service sector is an important consideration.

In economies experiencing deindustrialisation, the form this takes, as discussed in Rowthorn and Wells (1987) and Petit (1985), can have important implications for employment. To use the Rowthorn and Wells terminology, increases in the share of service employment can take two paths. One is that of 'positive' deindustrialisation where, in a growing economy with high wages and full employment, differential productivity growth means the share of service employment increases over time. The alternative is 'negative' deindustrialisation, where the increasing share of service employment takes place in a stagnant economy with low growth, low wages, and unemployment and is a feature of decline. Which of these paths an economy takes depends upon the dynamics of the industrial sector, and in the case of the UK it is the latter which seems the most realistic.

If manufacturing is in decline then the implications for the service sector need to be considered. To what extent is the growth in services dependent on the manufacturing base? To consider this question requires distinguishing those services which require manufacturing as an input and those that are intermediate outputs from final services. In addition, it is necessary to consider the potential for international trade in services. Many services are not easily tradeable and those that are, mainly producer services, have not tended to show the most employment growth.

Disaggregating service employment

It is clearly important to analyse the service sector in detail to identify the patterns and particular structure of growth in employment in the sector. Otherwise, we might fail to recognise changes in the structure of employment and the increasing importance of employment growth in industries we know little about, both of which might imply the need for profound changes in the workings of the labour market and the provision of education and training in the future. In addition, as the debate on deindustrialisation makes clear, it is dangerous to focus on the aggregate sectors, as this leads to a failure to recognise the heterogeneity of the service sector which, as mentioned above, can lead to over-optimistic assessments of its future prospects. Yet there have been suprisingly few attempts to analyse the changing structure of service employment at an industrial level and to work out the implications and potential uncertainties for future employment.

This chapter attempts to provide detailed information on the structure of service employment in the UK. It considers whether or not the service sector can provide the demand for labour which will compensate for the loss of employment in manufacturing. To answer such a question requires more than simply estimating the potential job creation in the service sector and comparing it to the likely job losses in manufacturing. The type of employment being created in the service sector will not necessarily match the characteristics of the labour being shed by manufacturing, there may be regional mismatches between demand and supply, and there may be changes in labour supply such that jobs created in the service sector are taken by persons not previously in the labour force. At a more general level, other sectors of the economy might be shedding labour at the same time, such as the public services, agriculture, or energy, which will affect the competition for employment in private services. Such factors can have important effects as they imply high levels of frictional unemployment, increasing long-term unemployment, skill bottlenecks and the possibility of high levels of vacancies coexisting with high unemployment. It is thus important to consider in detail the industries where employment is likely to be created, both to identify the sources of employment growth and the likely nature of the labour demanded.

The prospects for service employment

In considering the future prospects for service employment it is worth recognising the deficiencies of making simple extrapolations on the basis of industrial employment time series. Such an analysis is partial in nature and does not allow for feedbacks and constraints from the rest of the economy. This is a deficiency in both Robertson *et al.* (1982) and Rajan (1986), though the latter does integrate useful information from employer-based surveys.

This study is carried out within the framework provided by the Cambridge Econometrics (CE) 1986 forecast, using the Cambridge Growth Project model (Barker and Peterson, forthcoming). The model is a dynamic input-output structure integrated into a set of macroeconomic relationships, in which the major aggregate variables are computed, 'bottom-up', from industrial and commodity group detail. Thus, unlike other macroeconomic models, structural change within the economy can be studied within the consistent framework of the model. An alternative approach, such as NIESR (1986), uses an aggregate model to provide a 'top-down' forecast, but this approach cannot allow consistently for industrial change and feedback, which is clearly of importance in analysing structural change.

The approach adopted here is to use the CE industrial employment forecasts to examine the prospects for the service sector. While these forecasts have the advantage of being based upon a disaggregate model, they still share with other forecasts the presence of uncertainties. It is possible for structural breaks to invalidate the underlying assumptions of the model and the validity of the historically-estimated empirical relationships. It is, therefore, important to attempt to identify the possible sources of such uncertainty, and to consider the implications of such developments. The results of such an analysis will also help to inform the discussion of possible modernisation strategies for the UK as presented in Landesmann and Snell (1986).

Only the prospects for the private services are considered here. This is not to forget the importance of public sector employment but to accept that employment in public services is largely policy-determined. If the political will was there, public employment could be increased massively to soak up unemployment, although possibly at the expense of other economic problems. It is important to recognise, however, that the distinction between public and private services is not always straightforward, as some private services are publicly financed and some are dependent on public services e.g. private medicine.

The most detailed and reliable information available on the service industries is for employment, although the change from the 1968 to the 1980 SIC has caused difficulties. The reallocation of a number of the MLHs over the activity headings makes it impossible to create consistent detailed long-run data series. The problems of linking the industrial and activity heading data between the 1968 and the 1980 SICs are discussed in Kitson and Tarling (1986). In this study we use the data supplied by the *Department of Employment Gazette*, which provides consistent quarterly information from 1982.

An outline of the chapter

This chapter provides an analysis of the structure of service employment and its prospects at two levels. First, at a general analytical level where the development of the service sector is compared to that of other sectors and the interrelationships discussed. This is undertaken in Section 6.2, which looks at changes in employment of different sectors in the economy, and in Section 6.3 which focusses on the service industries. Second, the developments in the structure of service employment are sought at a more detailed disaggregate level in Section 6.4. This provides some extremely useful information, although in some industries highlighting the fact that we have little and inadequate information on some of the areas of high potential growth. While it is beyond the scope of the chapter to integrate the analysis at the two levels, Section 6.5 does attempt to draw some general conclusions and policy implications from both the general and the more specific trends identified.

6.2 Changes in manufacturing and service employment

Long-run trends

In analysing the development of employment in an economy it is important to distinguish long-run trends in the structure of employment from short-run changes. This is complicated by the fact that as changes in the structure of employment over time take place so must changes in the classifications used to record employment. Thus to study long-run trends of employment in empirical detail is extremely difficult, requiring numerous qualitative judgements. Robertson *et al.* (1982) present data for various years from 1841 onwards. After introducing the necessary caveats and warnings, however, the only substantive statements they can make are that it is not possible to trace the employment patterns of a particular industry over the whole period but that there are clear trends at an aggregate sectoral level. Considering primary (agriculture, forestry and fishing), secondary (mining, manufacturing, construction and utilities) and tertiary (the remaining services) sectors, it is clear that the primary sector has continually accounted for a smaller share of employment and the secondary sector has provided a relatively stable share of employment. In fact Rowthorn and Wells (1987) point out that this stability hides important developments in domestic services which tends to increase rapidly as a country industrialises and then to fall away as the country develops further.

Clearly the emergence of the service sector cannot be regarded as a recent development in most advanced economies. It is, however, a growth in the share of service employment that is observed and this is not necessarily associated with a loss of jobs in the secondary sector, or even with a declining secondary sector. It is important to recognise that such trends hide a great deal of structural change within the three sectors, and that the type of employment in the sectors has changed over time.

UK employment in the 1970s and 1980s

Considering more recent history, Robertson *et al.* (1982) argue that economic development in the period of the 1970s was not typical of the long-term developments. The contrasts of demand-led boom in 1973 and then the depression and unemployment with the higher oil prices, floating exchange rates, inflation and rising public expenditures, distinguish this period and influenced the structure of employment both directly and indirectly. Rowthorn and Wells (1987) deal with such considerations by distinguishing longer-term economic developments, upon which shorter-term business cycle effects can be transposed, and arguing that the pattern of foreign trade specialisation should be considered separately. Unlike most OECD countries, the UK has experienced massive changes in trade specialisation, from manufactures to oil and services, during the post-war period which has had a major impact on growth and employment structure. In the middle 1950s the UK had the most industrialised workforce in the capitalist world but since then has seen continuous decline.

Fig. 6.1 shows the trends identified in Robertson *et al.* (1982) to be continuing with the growth in service employment at the expense of primary industry, but also a marked fall in employment in manufacturing industry over the 1970s and 1980s. As Table 6.1 shows, there has also been a marked reduction in construction employment, the industry displaying its sensitivity to general growth and public expenditure over the period of the recession. It has also seen a marked increase in self-employment, 11 percentage points between 1980 and 1985. The only economic sector in which employment has continued to grow is in the service sector, both in absolute terms and as a proportion of total employment.

Figure 6.1   *Total employment by sector*

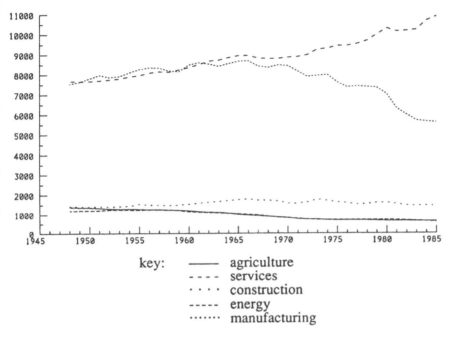

key: —— agriculture
        - - - - services
        · · · · construction
        - - - - - energy
        ········ manufacturing

Source: Institute for Employment Research and Cambridge Growth Project.

In the 1960s the net change in employment in services more than compensated for the fall in manufacturing employment, but in the 1970s it was not enough to prevent a fall in total employment. This situation has worsened in the 1980s. These developments, illustrated in Fig. 6.1, have important implications, as they show that the structure of employment is changing dramatically. There has been a marked decline in all sectors except services, the major losses being in manufacturing with its workforce of generally male full-time skilled and semi-skilled workers. As illustrated in Figs. 6.2 and 6.3, the service sector employment of males is in fact increasing, providing more male employment than manufacturing in the late 1970s, but the dominant trend in labour demand is increasingly for female workers and, as we shall see later, an increasing proportion of that female employment is part-time. The growth of female employment in the service sector has more than compensated for the loss of female employment in manufacturing.

Table 6.2 gives the sectoral employment forecast provided by Cambridge Econometrics (1986). These are based upon a more

Table 6.1   *Sectoral comparisons of UK employment (thousands)*

	1960	1970	1980	1985
1 Agriculture	1199.3	836.1	659.1	636.2
% female	14.8	17.8	19.5	18.3
% self-employed	33.2	37.9	38.7	40.1
Productivity[a]	6.5	11.6	18.3	21.4
2 Energy and water	1152.1	821.1	723.6	607.1
% female	6.0	9.5	12.8	13.5
% self-employed	0.0	0.0	0.0	0.0
Productivity[a]	17.8	32.1	54.9	65.1
3 Manufacturing	8492.5	8453.4	7036.4	5614.0
% female	32.0	30.3	29.3	28.6
% self-employed	1.3	1.6	2.0	3.3
Productivity[a]	12.6	17.6	22.2	25.4
4 Construction	1531.9	1582.8	1609.8	1431.5
% female	4.1	5.2	7.4	9.2
% self-employed	10.7	19.1	22.2	33.1
Productivity[a]	17.9	23.5	21.6	22.5
5 Services	8368.2	8869.2	10308.5	10897.5
% female	40.1	42.8	46.4	48.6
% self-employed	13.0	13.0	12.2	14.5
Productivity[a]	8.8	10.9	12.2	12.6

Proportions of total UK employment[b]

	1960	1970	1980	1985
1 Agriculture	5.9	4.1	3.2	3.3
2 Energy and water	5.7	4.0	3.6	3.2
3 Manufacturing	41.7	41.1	34.6	29.3
4 Construction	5.6	7.7	7.9	7.5
5 Services	41.0	43.2	50.7	56.8

Notes: [a] Productivity is measured as the output labour ratio.
         [b] Employees in employment plus self-employed.
Source: Institute for Employment Research and Cambridge Growth Project.

disaggregated industrial analysis, using the Cambridge Growth Project model, the results of which will be considered later. Clearly, the only potential for expansion of employment is in the service sector, which will provide 13 million jobs by the year 2000, three times that of manufacturing. If trends continue this also implies an increase in the proportion of self-employment, female and, by implication, part-time employment.

It would appear that there are a number of potential uncertainties to bear in mind when considering employment forecasts, because of the

Figure 6.2   *Total male employment by sector*

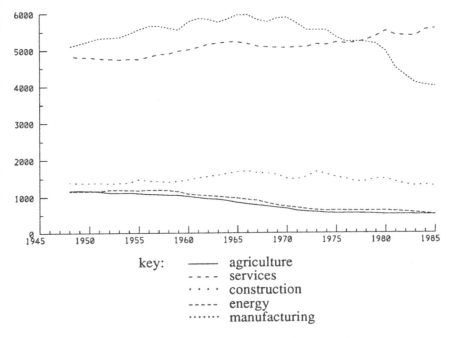

key: ———   agriculture
        - - - -   services
        · · · ·   construction
        - - - - -   energy
        ·······   manufacturing

Source: Institute for Employment Research and Cambridge Growth Project.

Table 6.2   *Sectoral forecasts of UK employment (thousands)*

	1985	1990	1995	2000
1 Agriculture	636	568	503	471
2 Energy and water	607	548	498	480
3 Manufacturing	5614	5482	5443	5557
4 Construction	1432	1483	1498	1554
5 Services	11264	12183	12718	13066

Note: The value for services in 1985 differs from Table 6.1 because it includes unallocated.
Source: *Cambridge Econometrics Forecast* (October 1986).

changing structure of employment. It is reasonable to argue that the growth in service employment may have less effect on the level of unemployment than might be expected because of the changing structure

Figure 6.3 *Total female employment by sector*

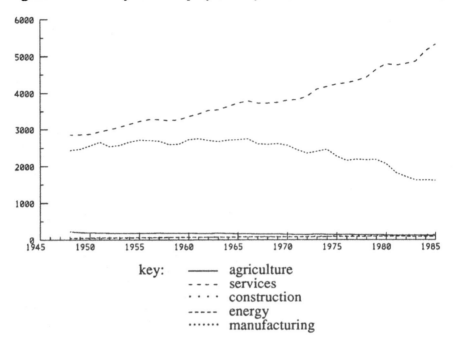

key: ——— agriculture
      - - - - services
      · · · · construction
      - - - - - energy
      ······· manufacturing

Source: Institute for Employment Research and Cambridge Growth Project.

of skill demand and changing participation rates. Part-time jobs are often taken by women, or young people, who were not registered as unemployed, and so increases in employment need not affect the number of long-term unemployed. Such developments can have drastic implications. There may be further substantial changes in the type of employment demanded, new skills could become obsolete quickly, and it is possible that some of the greatest growth areas might have the highest potential for labour-shedding technical progress.

A further important consideration is the level of dependence of service employment on manufacturing. Much service sector employment is not final output and not tradeable. The future of services could be dependent on the future of manufacturing if the growth is mainly in domestically-consumed intermediate services. The service industries are, however, heterogeneous and to consider such developments adequately needs more detailed information, to which we now turn.

6.3 Employment in the service industries

Previous work

A detailed analysis of service employment, based on the 1968 SIC classifications, was undertaken by Robertson *et al.* (1982) for the first half of the 1970s. They distinguished transport and communication, distributive trades, insurance finance and banking, professional and scientific, and miscellaneous services, together with public administration, and found that the biggest increase in employment was in professional and scientific services for women. This is seen to be largely the result of the expansion of health and education services. Only transport and communications showed a decline in employment (actually reflecting a fall in most of its MLH headings), while distributive trades showed an almost constant employment level and all other groups had growth in employment, particularly public administration.

Employment growth in services 1960-1985

Table 6.3 gives a breakdown of the service industries employment over the period 1960 to 1985 using data consistent with the 1980 SIC. This shows similar patterns of employment growth, although it does not include public administration. The transport industries show little growth in employment, and communications, while being an industry of high growth, is also one of high productivity growth and so has shown little employment growth. The main growth in employment has been that of over 100,000 in distribution, with hotels and catering, business services and miscellaneous services also showing significant growth. All of these industries have more than 40 per cent women employees and for all of them that proportion is growing.

In 1985 distribution employed about 4 million people, almost 50 per cent of them women and over 15 per cent self-employed. Productivity growth was reasonably slow, but it is important to remember that the productivity measures reported in Table 6.3 are simply the output-employment ratios and, for many service industries, where some components of output may be estimated from employment, they are of questionable value. The hotels and catering industry has almost doubled its employment over the last 25 years: by 1985 it employed over 1 million people of whom around 60 per cent were women and around 15 per cent self-employed.

Table 6.3   *UK employment in service industries (thousands)*

	1960	1970	1980	1985
1 Distribution etc.	3646.3	3611.2	3894.8	4059.6
% female	43.8	53.3	52.5	52.3
% self-employed	17.6	16.4	14.3	15.9
Productivity	7.9	9.6	9.7	10.6
2 Hotels and catering	777.6	849.5	1116.6	1226.3
% female	58.6	57.9	62.7	62.2
% self-employed	14.4	15.8	12.2	13.6
Productivity	8.9	9.7	8.5	7.9
3 Rail transport	367.8	212.4	183.0	148.2
% female	7.7	6.7	7.1	6.1
% self-employed	0.0	0.0	0.0	0.0
Productivity	5.8	8.5	9.3	10.8
4 Other land transport	568.1	592.7	552.7	487.4
% female	11.3	10.4	11.5	11.1
% self-employed	7.2	9.9	17.8	18.7
Productivity	9.2	11.6	13.4	17.4
5 Sea, air and other	393.1	372.3	410.0	335.5
% female	11.3	18.0	26.1	28.5
% self-employed	0.0	0.0	0.0	3.9
Productivity	17.1	25.3	29.3	36.5
6 Communications	344.9	436.0	439.0	435.6
% female	25.5	25.3	24.8	25.9
% self-employed	0.0	0.0	0.5	0.9
Productivity	8.9	11.8	17.3	21.4
7 Business services	1101.3	1478.8	1879.7	2239.1
% female	38.7	43.0	44.5	45.4
% self-employed	10.8	10.5	9.7	11.9
Productivity	9.0	10.3	13.4	14.6
8 Miscellaneous services	1238.9	1383.8	1838.4	2120.6
% female	53.7	54.4	60.2	62.5
% self-employed	19.8	20.0	15.6	22.6
Productivity	9.4	10.8	10.3	11.4

Note: Productivity measured as output employment ratio.
Source: Institute for Employment Research and Cambridge Growth Project.

Forecasts of services employment

The Cambridge Econometrics forecast, presented in Table 6.4, shows no growth in transport employment and, despite high output growth in communications, high productivity prevents any significant employment growth in the industry. The main growth is forecast to be in distribution,

Table 6.4   *Forecasts of UK employment in service industries (thousands)*

	1985	1990	1995	2000
1 Distribution etc.	4036	4287	4400	4504
2 Hotels and catering	1223	1372	1456	1500
3 Rail transport	146	123	111	108
4 Other land transport	494	518	501	460
5 Sea, air and other	334	291	333	369
6 Communications	431	462	456	469
7 Business services	2189	2508	2648	2762
8 Miscellaneous services	2018	2161	2339	2420
Total	19553	20262	20667	21143

Source: *Cambridge Econometrics Forecast* (October 1986).

hotels and catering, business services and miscellaneous services, which provide over 11 million new jobs by 1990. We shall now consider the developments on these industries in more detail.

Distribution

Distribution shows steady growth in employment with high output growth, above that of GDP, over the forecast period. The recent high growth rate is considered to represent substitution for manufacturers own distribution networks, which cannot go on indefinitely. The main component of demand is consumer demand (mainly retailing) which is about double that of industrial demand, although in terms of growth consumer demand is expected to tail off in the medium to long run. The industry is extremely important both because of the high level of employment it supports and because it can account for 15-25 per cent of the purchase price of some goods. As Fig. 6.4 shows, distribution has always contained a high proportion of self-employed workers and is likely to continue to do so. Female employment accounts for around half of the labour force in the industry, though this is possibly changing with the reduction of job opportunities elsewhere for males. The high proportion of women is, however, related to the high proportion of part-time employment and both are unlikely to change given the high growth of part-time employment in the industry.

Table 6.5 shows the structure of employment for employees in employment in distribution in GB. Employment in the industry increased

Figure 6.4 *Employment in distribution and repair*

Source: *Department of Employment Gazette.*

by around 400,000 between 1982 and 1985. The proportion of females employed increased slightly and the proportion of part-time employees increased by around 6 percentage points. The constituent industries maintained reasonably constant shares of employment, with the trends in female and part-time employment identified in the aggregate still applicable at the more disaggregate level.

There is clearly great variety within the industry. Some products require local outlets, as they are heavy and difficult to transport or need to be tailored to specification. In contrast, light consumer goods can best be dealt with in a more centralised manner, possibly at a national level. The output of the industry is measured mainly as the margins earned on the activities, with distribution exports being largely margins earned on imported goods and distribution imports, margins on exported goods.

The major development in the industry has been the increase in control retailing organisations have been achieving over the distribution of their products with their increased buying power. This has led to an increase in efficiency and flexibility through the use of centralised warehouse systems and the resulting reduction in required stockholdings

Table 6.5   *Distribution, employees in employment, GB*

		December 1982			December 1985		
		(a)	(b)	(c)	(a)	(b)	(c)
Distribution		3099.7	51.1	51.9	3487.0	51.6	58.3
61	Wholesale	27.4	31.1	31.8	27.6	31.7	40.4
611	Agric., textile, raw mat.	1.0	28.0	32.5	0.9	31.0	43.9
612	Fuels, ores, metals etc.	3.2	23.5	25.2	3.2	24.0	31.4
613	Timber, building mats	3.9	24.2	30.6	3.8	24.8	39.3
614	Machinery, ind. equip.	4.4	26.8	26.4	4.4	26.8	31.6
615	Household hardware	1.7	36.1	31.0	1.7	36.4	40.3
616	Textiles, clothing, food	1.2	47.0	34.2	1.3	48.4	42.3
617	Food, drink, tobacco	7.7	31.5	37.6	7.6	31.8	46.6
618	Pharmac., medical	1.0	49.5	24.0	0.9	48.4	36.1
619	Other wholesale	3.4	38.6	32.4	3.6	38.7	43.2
62	Scrap and waste mat.	0.6	18.6	47.1	0.6	16.9	66.7
63	Commission agents	0.6	38.4	34.8	0.6	37.6	48.0
64/5	Retail	65.2	62.7	56.5	65.1	63.2	62.4
641	Food	18.0	63.6	62.1	18.3	63.9	70.8
642	Confectioners etc.	4.9	68.0	70.2	4.8	67.0	72.8
643	Chemists	4.2	86.6	43.2	3.9	86.5	44.2
645	Clothing	4.9	77.7	56.8	5.1	78.5	60.2
646	Footwear, leather	1.9	83.3	62.5	2.2	84.3	74.6
647	Furnishings	0.7	45.4	68.9	0.7	51.0	67.4
648	Household hardware	5.5	46.6	53.9	5.5	49.1	64.5
651	Motor vehicle parts	5.8	23.9	37.0	5.6	23.2	40.0
652	Filling stations	2.5	30.6	43.6	2.3	33.5	57.8
653	Books/stationers	2.1	60.4	65.0	2.1	60.1	61.3
654	Other specialised	3.2	56.0	45.0	3.4	56.9	55.0
656	Mixed retail	11.6	78.0	53.7	11.2	78.0	57.4
67	Repair	6.2	20.5	44.5	6.2	22.9	51.6
671	Motor vehicles	5.3	19.2	45.2	5.3	21.3	52.4
672/3	Footwear/leather	0.9	28.6	41.8	0.9	32.4	49.0

Notes: (a) Percentage of total for categories.
(b) Percentage of females.
(c) Percentage of females who work part-time.
Source: *Department of Employment Gazette.*

at the outlet. These developments continue to erode the viability of the manufacturers' own distribution networks. There is still great scope for further cost-saving and increased flexibility, with increased mechanisation and the use of information technology and outside specialist consultants. The retail industry has continued to boom with continuous growth in sales. Retailing now employs around 2 million workers in a quarter of a million outlets. There has been an increase in concentration, and design, presentation and quality in both goods and the stores themselves have become increasingly important; this is likely to continue to be the case. A further major development has been the move to out-of-town premises and hypermarkets, leaving the high street to smaller specialist shops and increasing the importance and popularity of local convenience shops.

Technological development in the industry is rapid and the adoption of 'electronic fund transfers at the point of sale' and the general move towards a cashless society implies further potential for productivity growth especially in retailing, which will continue the patterns of change in employment. Smith and Hitchens (1985) compared the UK retail and wholesale industry with that of the US and Germany. They found productivity growth in the UK to be relatively low, which they attributed in part to the comparatively low standard of living. They concluded that there was certainly potential for productivity growth in the UK.

The distribution industry is an important employer and is likely to remain so, yet there are clear uncertainties regarding its importance for the future provision of employment. Both retail and wholesale distribution are clearly dependent on manufacturing and manufacturing imports, and are open to potentially profound technological change which could reduce employment massively or change the structure of the labour force further. At present the industry employs a high proportion of female, part-time workers especially in retailing and there is a high proportion of self-employed. Further casualisation of the labour force is highly probable.

Hotels and catering

The hotel and catering industry is forecast to have high growth, tailing off in the medium term to around 1.5 per cent p.a. Productivity growth is slow so the industry provides almost 300,000 extra jobs by the year 2000. The personal nature of many of the services implies relatively little scope for labour shedding. In 1985 the industry employed just over a million people but, as can be seen from Table 6.6 and Fig. 6.5, 65 per cent of the employees were female and 75 per cent of these were part-time employed, for GB. This represents an increase of 5 percentage points in the proportion of females employed part-time between 1982 and 1985. Often these part-time female workers are employed for limited hours to keep them below the national insurance threshold. The work is often seasonal with a significant reduction in jobs and/or average hours at the end of the season although, with increasing leisure-

Figure 6.5   *Employment in hotels and catering*

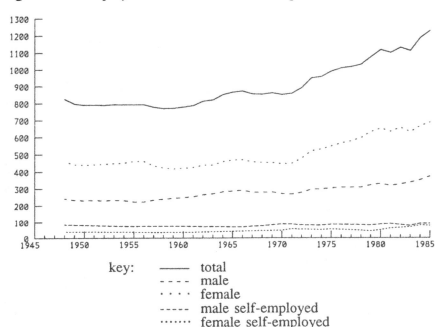

key: ────── total
            ─ ─ ─ ─ male
            · · · · female
            ─ ─ ─ ─ male self-employed
            ······· female self-employed

Source: *Department of Employment Gazette.*

facility provision, conferences, winter breaks etc., the hours could become more evenly spread over the year. The hotel trade and public houses both employ about 25 per cent of total employment in the industry, though the latter has a higher proportion of female employment and a substantially higher proportion of part-time employees.

There is also great heterogeneity in employment requirements and shift patterns. Full-time jobs are usually confined to administration and management. The labour force is generally low-skilled (although there are of course many skilled jobs), poorly qualified and with little unionisation outside local authorities and the NHS.

The prospects for this industry depend upon a number of rather volatile factors, namely trends, fashions and attitudes. Tourism can be influenced by the behaviour of the exchange rate, which depends in turn on the price of oil, and by the international situation. There is also the problem of the concentration of tourists in London, which tends to lead to localised capacity constraints. Fortunately, corporate business demand is less volatile and is of increasing importance to most hotel-group business, especially off-season. There has been some shift in eating

Table 6.6   *Hotels and catering, employees in employment, GB*

		December 1982			December 1985		
		(a)	(b)	(c)	(a)	(b)	(c)
66	Hotels and catering	856.1	66.5	70.6	1003.7	65.2	74.8
661	Restaurants, cafes etc.	19.8	62.2	68.1	18.9	61.6	71.1
662	Public houses, bars	25.9	72.0	85.2	25.6	69.9	91.1
663	Nightclubs etc.	16.0	62.9	81.5	15.6	60.2	88.2
664	Canteens, messes	12.6	76.0	58.4	12.2	72.7	61.2
665	Hotel trade	24.0	63.0	54.6	25.1	63.8	59.9
667	Other tourist etc. accommod.	1.7	43.2	81.2	2.5	52.2	65.6

Notes: (a) Percentage of total for categories.
        (b) Percentage of females.
        (c) Percentage of females who work part-time.
Source: *Department of Employment Gazette.*

habits which has influenced the structure of employment in the industry, with the growth of fast-food outlets and the shift to healthier food. Changes in technology (e.g. freezers and microwave ovens) have increased the number of institutions that can provide food.

The hotel and catering industry is, therefore, going through a number of important developments and it is not clear what the final outcome will be nor whether technological development will reduce employment or not. It seems likely that the already high proportion of part-time female employment will continue to increase and, though some skilled jobs will remain, technology will further reduce the level of skill. Further casualisation of the workforce is likely. There is great potential for food production to be undertaken by manufacturing industry, with catering simply providing a service. This would reduce employment potential and skill levels, and mean the scope for labour shedding is greater than anticipated.

Business services

Business services are forecast to be the area of most growth in the economy. Output, which is dominated by intermediate demands, has a long-run growth of around 4.5 per cent, although net output shows a marked tail-off in growth. It is clear that the best prospects are in intermediate business services. Productivity growth is high, reflecting the great potential for further introduction of computer and information technology to increase efficiency. The increasing internationalisation of business services is mainly reflected in sales abroad. Exports show strong growth, while imports in contrast are relatively unimportant.

Figure 6.6   *Employment in business services*

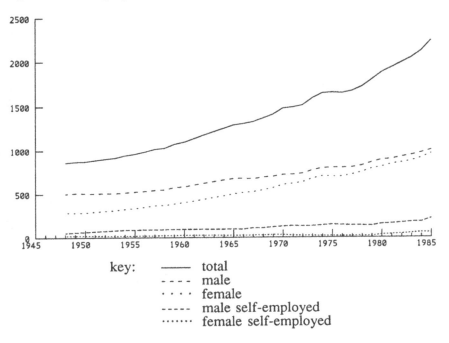

key: —— total
       - - - - male
       · · · · female
       - - - - - male self-employed
       ······· female self-employed

Source: *Department of Employment Gazette.*

As Fig. 6.6 shows, there is a high and increasing proportion of females employed in the industry, but these aggregates hide a great deal of variation within the constituent components of the industry. Table 6.7 gives the breakdown of the business services industry in Great Britain, together with details of employees in employment and the sex and part-time structure of employment in the subgroups. It employed almost 2 million people in 1985 and has good prospects for growth in employment. There are, however, radical changes in the structure of the industry taking place, both in the UK and abroad, with rapid movements towards concentration, conglomeration and internationalisation.

Banking and financial services represent over a quarter of the employment in business services, with over 20 per cent in banking and just under 7 per cent in other financial institutions. These are holding their share of growing total employment. Both of these categories have

Table 6.7 *Business services, employees in employment, GB*

		December 1983			December 1985		
		(a)	(b)	(c)	(a)	(b)	(c)
8	Banking, finance, insurance	1842.9	48.4	28.0	1988.7	48.7	31.3
81	Banking and finance	27.5	57.8	20.3	26.8	58.0	24.5
814	Banking, bill discounting	20.9	56.6	16.9	20.1	56.6	21.0
815	Other fin. instits	6.6	61.6	30.4	6.7	62.2	33.7
82	Insurance	12.5	43.2	17.3	12.6	42.6	18.1
83	Business services	49.5	47.9	34.7	50.2	48.2	37.2
831	Aux to bank and fin.	1.2	42.2	22.8	1.3	40.4	24.3
832	Aux to insurance	3.7	53.0	31.6	4.0	54.0	37.0
834	House and estate agents	4.3	55.6	44.0	4.3	57.7	46.5
837	Prof. services n.e.s.	10.0	30.3	38.1	10.2	30.7	37.8
838	Advertising	2.2	44.6	29.2	2.0	48.0	32.1
8394	Computer services	3.1	30.9	22.6	3.3	30.8	25.5
8395	Business services n.e.s.	9.1	49.8	41.8	9.8	49.6	43.6
8396	Cent. office not alloc.	2.3	36.4	16.4	2.0	35.2	19.6
84	Renting moveables	5.0	26.8	31.3	4.9	28.1	36.5
842	Construction mach. etc.	2.2	13.8	47.3	2.1	14.0	41.4
846	Consumer goods	1.6	38.4	33.6	1.5	42.2	40.3
841/3/8/9	Trans. and moveable	1.3	34.2	23.5	1.3	34.6	28.3
85	Real estate	5.5	37.1	36.7	5.4	40.9	43.9

Notes: (a) Percentage of total for categories.
         (b) Percentage of females.
         (c) Percentage of females who work part-time.
Source: *Department of Employment Gazette.*

over 50 per cent female employment and even over the two years 1983-5 show a marked increase in the proportion of employed females who are part-time.

The major consideration for the prospects of banking and financial services is the effect of deregulation. Despite high growth and optimism, the breaking down of old barriers exposes the institutions to dangers as well as opportunities. Technology is changing banks, as Cooke (1986) describes in detail. Improved communications and microtechnology mean that branches are becoming more efficient. With cash machines transactions take place more quickly, information can be processed more readily, and cheques can be cleared electronically, thus reducing payroll and premises costs. These developments could have significant effects on the structure of employment, increasing flexibility with automatic branches and possibly leading to a cashless society. This in turn would have important implications for distribution. There is certainly great potential for the application of labour-saving technology and it is likely that the increased flexibility will mean the trend towards female part-time employment will continue.

Half of the employment in the business services industry is in fact under the business services heading. All of these have relatively high, and generally increasing proportions of female employees, and even over the two years a relatively large shift towards the women employees being part-timers. Under the business services heading, professional and technical services is a major growth area, a beneficiary of the reduction of in-house resources by manufacturing firms. These are mainly medium-sized companies, in which the development of such capabilities is particularly prone to closure in recessions. There has been more and more technical specialisation and use of new technology, but many firms had already been using consultants before, so there has not been a significant growth in the client base. Instead, there has been an increase in the allocation of resources and an increase in content and unit costs as managers recognise the importance of presentation and marketing. Among consultants there has been an increase in the expertise of the workforce and an increase in the number of specialised consultancies. The employment structure is extremely flexible and may be project-related, management-related, or both, depending upon the mix of administration and development.

The prospects for the business service industries are good but there is great variety. The design and advertising industries are fragmented and difficult to define, containing large multidisciplinary companies and small specialist ones, to cover the disparate disciplines that make up the industries. The leading UK companies are more successful than their continental European rivals, and the demand from overseas makes them influential internationally and implies good prospects of future expansion.

Computing services have seen extremely high growth and have become an important international business, with US companies dominating developments and European firms having to work hard to develop home markets and expand abroad. Computing services used to be divided into software, processing, consultancy, and recruitment and training, but falling hardware prices and increasing sophistication of machines at the cheap end have led to the distinctions becoming blurred. This has also created a demand for more sophisticated software that can be run on companies' own microcomputers, although software for mainframes is still the mainstay of the market. The market is certainly becoming more volatile, with a slow-down in capital spending, increased price sensitivity in the mainframe database market, a tendency for companies to diversify and offer a broader range of products, and the dominating influence of IBM.

As Table 6.7 shows, not only are prospects good for the industry on the basis of recent developments but there are also clear changes in the structure of the workforce. Of further interest is the fact that the heterogeneous headings professional services n.e.s., business services n.e.s. and central office not allocated, contain almost 22 per cent of total employment in this group of industries. In other words, a sizeable and growing proportion of service employment is in categories which are not particularly well-defined. There is the additional uncertainty about the prospects for the industry in determining to what extent the demand is simply the result of manufacturing firms shedding departments and using consultants. Most of the industries appear to be heavily dependent on manufacturing industry in producing intermediate goods, though the categories vary markedly in their potential to be tradeable. There are great uncertainties surrounding the future prospects of the components of this industry. In terms of employment, technology could lead to a high level of labour shedding and deskilling, implying low employment growth despite high growth in the industry. Profound structural changes in labour demand could occur with changing skill requirements.

Miscellaneous services

The miscellaneous services industry is a heterogeneous collection of services which employed around 2 million people in 1985, second only to distribution. Because of changing social attitudes towards health, leisure and recreation it contains categories with high potential for growth. At the same time, however, the prospects for this important employer clearly depend upon future movements in the exchange rate, the related volume of foreign tourists, developments in broadcasting and changes in attitudes and lifestyles. Unfortunately, many components are vulnerable to fast-changing fashions and trends. The forecast for miscellaneous services shows growth above that of GDP, nearly 4 per cent in 1987 but tailing off to around 2.5 per cent in the longer term. More than half the output is net output, with consumer demand dominating industrial demand. Trade in miscellaneous services is not particularly important.

In common with the other services there are problems in measuring the output of miscellaneous services, and these problems are made worse by their heterogeneity. A large proportion of the output of personal services can only practically be measured by the labour input. This leads to difficulties in interpreting changes in productivity, as increases in efficiency and reductions in quality can be observationally equivalent. Clearly, the total figures for this category will reflect different trends, increasing productivity, increasing quality and changes in the nature of the service.

Table 6.8   *Miscellaneous services, employees in employment, GB*

		December 1982			December 1985		
		(a)	(b)	(c)	(a)	(b)	(c)
	Miscellaneous services	1329.2	60.1	54.2	1451.4	63.2	54.9
921	Refuse disposal etc.	6.2	13.7	40.4	5.5	13.0	41.8
94	Research and development	8.8	27.5	16.8	9.4	29.8	14.8
96	Other services	42.2	76.3	62.2	43.9	78.5	62.3
961	Social welfare etc.	34.7	82.1	64.7	36.8	83.5	64.2
969	Tourist and other ser.	2.7	53.7	52.9	2.4	57.3	64.0
97	Recreational, cultural	30.1	50.4	55.3	28.9	54.3	56.8
971/6	Film prodn, authors	2.1	47.0	59.7	1.9	58.0	68.1
974	Radio, TV, theatres	5.2	39.5	29.4	5.1	44.0	27.2
977	Libraries	3.9	65.5	41.5	4.1	69.3	38.9
979	Sport, other recreation	18.8	50.6	64.2	17.8	53.4	67.9
98	Personal services	12.6	74.7	36.2	12.4	76.8	37.6
981	Laundries etc.	4.5	70.7	41.4	4.5	73.0	43.0
982	Hairdressing etc.	6.5	87.6	31.0	6.2	88.9	32.3
989	Personal services n.e.s.	1.7	35.7	58.8	1.7	42.7	52.8

Notes: (a) Percentage of total for categories.
         (b) Percentage of females.
         (c) Percentage of females who work part-time.
Source: *Department of Employment Gazette.*

Unfortunately the figures in Table 6.8, for employees in employment in GB, do not correspond directly to the aggregate figures used previously. Because of the difficulty of treating the public sector, some approximation and compensating inclusions and exclusions were made in deriving the figures. They do, however, give a reasonable idea of the structure of employment within the industry. In 1985 almost 1.5 million persons were employed in these sub-industries and, as shown in Fig. 6.7, over 60 per cent of these were female and over half of the female employees were part-time. The proportion of females increased by 3 percentage points between 1982 and 1985, while the proportion of them employed part-time remained reasonably constant. The shares in employment of the different categories remained fairly constant but there have been a number of changes in the structure. Film production etc.,

Figure 6.7   *Employment in miscellaneous services*

key: ——   total
            - - - -   male
            · · · ·   female
            - - - - -   male self-employed
            ·······   female self-employed

Source: *Department of Employment Gazette.*

saw a small reduction in employment but a relatively large change in the proportion of female employees. Libraries saw a fall in the proportion of females employed part-time and there was a 6 percentage point fall in the proportion of women employed part-time in personal services n.e.s., though the proportion of women employed increased.

Recreational and cultural services represent around 30 per cent of the employment in miscellaneous services. The UK leisure industry is growing rapidly and is likely to continue expanding. Tourist facilities are likely to face increased demand and have already seen increased investment, as foreign tourists benefit from the exchange-rate depreciation and domestic tourists take more short and off-season holidays.

There are in fact continuing regional and social differences in affluence and attitude in the UK. Leisure interests are generally fragmenting and a greater role is played by fashion, health-consciousness and a desire for more informal leisure pursuits. There is an increasing demand for participatory leisure activities, and this has led to increased provision for health, sport and other recreational facilities by private as well public investment in sports halls in urban areas. Film and television are a very important component of trade in miscellaneous services and have generally shown a trade surplus. Personal services represent around 12 per cent of employment, mainly in laundries and hairdressing. Their employment would probably be larger if the self-employed were also considered.

6.4 Regional distribution of service employment

The spatial distribution of employment in the service industries is clearly of great importance. Any forecast of employment growth will have a major uncertainty attached to the regional distribution of labour demand. A high growth of service employment in prosperous regions will not be much use to the poorer regions. In addition, migration might be infeasible because of, for example, house-price differentials, leading to frictional unemployment.

Table 6.9 shows the structure of employment for the service industries across the regions for 1971, 1980 and 1985. The figures refer to employees in employment and the industrial categories are more aggregated than those discussed previously. Distribution and hotel and catering are combined and public administration is included in other services.

The most striking feature of this table is the stability in the distribution of the employment of each industry across the regions since 1971. The first part of the table shows the share of the region's employment in each industry as a share of the total UK employment for that industry. In no region did the share change by more than 2 percentage points over the 15-year period. There is, however, no stability in the share of the industry employment in a region in the total employment of that region. All of the three industry groups have employed an increasing proportion of the regional workforce.

It would thus appear that, while service employment has increased in importance for all regions, the actual distribution of employment across those regions has been stable. This might imply the importance of regional income in supporting services and the lack of inter-regional and international tradeable goods within the service industries, and thus implicitly their dependence on manufacturing and compensating public expenditure flows, such as benefit payments. It certainly implies that services are unlikely to provide compensatory employment growth in the regions as manufacturing declines.

Table 6.9 *Regional distribution of employment, employees in employment*

| | Share of region in UK employment for the industry (%) | | | | | | | | |
| | Hotel and catering | | | Banking, finance and insurance | | | Public admin. other services | | |
	1971	1980	1985	1971	1980	1985	1971	1980	1985
SE	35.8	34.2	34.4	51.6	48.6	48.7	37.4	35.0	35.5
EA	2.8	3.2	3.7	2.2	2.6	2.6	2.8	3.0	3.1
SW	7.2	8.3	8.1	4.6	6.5	6.5	6.6	7.2	7.4
EM	5.2	6.1	5.8	3.7	4.4	4.6	5.0	5.6	5.5
WM	8.5	8.5	8.8	6.5	7.1	7.0	8.0	8.1	7.4
N	5.5	5.2	4.6	3.4	3.5	3.3	5.3	5.0	4.9
NW	11.7	11.1	11.2	10.5	9.6	9.8	11.2	11.0	11.2
Y&H	7.9	8.4	8.3	5.8	6.1	6.2	7.4	7.7	7.4
W	3.8	3.9	4.0	2.8	2.9	2.7	4.6	4.8	4.9
S	9.5	9.2	9.4	7.6	7.4	7.4	9.1	9.5	9.6
NI	2.0	1.8	1.7	1.4	1.5	1.3	2.5	3.2	3.2
	Share of the industry in total regional employment (%)								
	1971	1980	1985	1971	1980	1985	1971	1980	1985
SE	17.9	19.7	21.0	9.4	11.0	13.1	25.6	29.0	30.4
EA	17.4	19.6	23.0	4.8	6.2	7.3	23.6	25.8	26.9
SW	20.0	22.5	23.4	4.7	6.9	8.2	25.2	28.0	29.6
EM	14.1	17.1	18.1	3.7	4.8	6.4	18.4	22.4	24.0
WM	14.2	16.6	20.3	3.9	5.4	7.0	18.3	22.7	23.9
N	16.4	18.4	20.1	3.7	4.9	6.2	21.8	25.4	29.6
NW	15.8	18.3	21.0	5.1	6.1	8.1	20.7	25.9	29.3
Y&H	15.4	18.3	21.1	4.1	5.2	6.9	19.8	24.0	26.3
W	14.6	16.8	19.6	3.8	4.9	5.8	24.2	29.5	33.9
S	17.5	19.0	21.6	5.1	6.0	7.4	22.8	28.3	30.9
NI	15.4	15.0	16.1	3.8	5.1	5.6	26.2	38.5	43.6
UK	16.6	18.8	20.8	6.0	7.4	9.1	22.8	27.0	29.2

Source: *Department of Employment Gazette.*

6.5 Conclusions

A full integration of the detail provided in the previous section with the more general analysis of the earlier sections would be a book in its own right. All we can hope to do here is to present some general conclusions which are informed by the more detailed analysis.

Importance of service employment

Overall, the forecasts for the service industries imply that employment in distribution, hotels and catering, business and miscellaneous services will be of increasing importance in the future. If trends continue this seems to imply an increase in the availability of female, and by implication, part-time employment, and an increase in self-employment. It also has implications for the required skills of the labour force. These industries demand skills and experience or flexibility very different from the characteristics of those workers who continue to be shed by manufacturing. This will be true whether the shift to service employment is in the context of a healthy manufacturing base or a declining one. There is uncertainty about whether the labour market can adjust to accommodate these structural changes and indeed whether the social infrastructure of training and education is adequate.

Some weaknesses of employment growth in services

The detailed information on the structure of the industry underlines these trends and at the same time introduces some further concerns. It is apparent that there are structural changes in the nature of the service industries taking place and that we know very little about some of the sub-industries in which strongest employment growth is taking place. Another concern is the extent to which the growth in service employment is just substitution for loss of employment in manufacturing, through industry farming out services which were previously produced internally. This would mean that much of the growth is only one off, pertinent to the recession, and not sustainable. While it is possible for the share of service employment to grow regardless of the state of manufacturing, through 'positive' or 'negative' deindustrialisation, the prospects for total employment are clearly affected by which path is taken. The scope for services to provide employment in a stagnant economy will be determined by the level of dependence of services on manufacturing, through their being goods-related services or intermediate in nature, and the potential for international trade in services.

From the detailed analysis of the sector what at first appears to be healthy growth becomes more suspect. Many services with potential for growth are dependent on manufacturing, being goods-related; some growth evident in retailing, for instance, is dependent on imports, while growth in others, such as many business services, is dependent on intermediate demand. Some of the employment growth is clearly substitution from formerly internalised manufacturing activities, while many of the sub-industries are amenable to high productivity growth, particularly producer services, making the prospects for future employment growth poor. The potential for trade in many services is low and, while a number are potentially tradeable, they are not necessarily exportable. This seems to be the case for many of the services which have high potential for employment growth, while others depend on volatile demand factors, introducing great uncertainty into any predictions.

While there are some tendencies to commercialise domestically-produced services, forces are acting in the other direction (as Gershuny argues) to provide 'self service' by the use of manufactured goods. This evidence points to a high level of dependence of service employment on the manufacturing sector.

Apart from a detailed analysis of developments in the service industries, this chapter has attempted to identify uncertainties in industrial forecasts made within the consistent framework of a disaggregate 'bottom-up' macroeconomic model. This is not to criticise the forecasts, which are superior to the simple extrapolations used in some previous studies. Rather, any forecast is dependent on the information available and, as that is of course historical or possibly of questionable accuracy, structural changes can invalidate forecasts based on such information. Thus the results of the detailed analysis indicate where the underlying assumptions and historical information inherent in the model may be suspect. The changing structure of employment implies great changes in the labour force and places requirements on education and training. The implications of the analysis are that the forecasts might, if anything, be over-optimistic. They imply a belief that the social infrastructure required for the changes to take place will be forthcoming in a manner which will not put strains on the labour market. If, as seems likely, this does not happen, high levels of frictional employment, skill shortages and the creation of a lost generation of long-term unemployed ex-manufacturing workers could be the result.

The nature of the work provided in the service sector has profound implications for future employment. We have seen increases in part-time and female employment, and Rajan (1986) identifies an increase in the employment of young persons in services. These characteristics have meant an increase in the employment of those not registered as unemployed, with increasing female participation rates. Though there are some highly skilled jobs, much of the employment growth is in low skilled occupations. There is also a high level of self-employment in personal services and an increasing casualisation of much of the labour force.

A further question is whether the generally low productivity of the service sector will be maintained. It is clear that there is considerable scope for productivity improvements in some industries through the introduction of information technology. There is certainly the possibility of zero employment growth in a dynamic financial services sector. In such service industries the potential for the application of new technology to increase productivity, displace labour and change skill requirements could well be greater than that seen in manufacturing industry.

In addition, there is the important problem of the regional distribution of service employment. There is little potential for the development of inter-regional or international tradeable services in the regions, with most service employment more related to regional incomes. Service employment is unlikely to be able to provide a solution to regional unemployment and it is likely that the focus of services employment growth will remain the prosperous South East.

Policy implications

The policy implications of these conclusions are that services are linked to the manufacturing sector. A healthy manufacturing sector, even though having a reduced share of employment, is important to the potential for growth in service employment. Within the service sector there are numerous developments in the structure of employment which have important implications. It seems likely that policies on education and training will be needed to give flexibility to the labour force, by allowing workers to retrain throughout their working lives, as their skills become obsolete. Education thus becomes more important than targeted vocational training because of rapidly changing skill requirements. In addition, it is likely that the problem of long-term unemployment will get worse and some new initiatives, which take account of the regional dimension, will be required. If we are not to see high levels of frictional unemployment in the future a high level of investment in social infrastructure is clearly required.

7

BANKING AND CHANGES IN INDUSTRY STRUCTURE

David Williams[*]

7.1 Introduction

The period since 1979 has witnessed major changes to the structure of British manufacturing industry, as companies have been forced to compete in a more hostile environment. As a result, industry is generally perceived to be leaner and fitter, although economists of differing persuasions continue to debate the extent to which greater efficiency is the result of uncompetitive capacity being rationalised, or whether working practices and plant efficiencies have genuinely been improved.[1] The attention received by the manufacturing sector has become more focussed as declining oil revenues have become a reality and there are indications that manufacturing output growth remains disappointing.

Whilst the emphasis placed on the changes taking place in manufacturing is understandable, it is possible to argue that since 1982 banking has experienced changes of a similar, if not greater magnitude, leading up to the start of the so-called Big Bang. Although the changes now taking place will have widespread effects, spilling over into all of the major financial markets, it is the changes which impact on the relationship between the commercial banks and their major corporate borrowers which is of particular interest to the work of the industrial economists in the City of London. This paper seeks to identify the

[*] The Midland Bank is not necessarily in agreement with the views expressed in this paper. The author is grateful to Dennis Turner for his comments on earlier drafts.
[1] For discussion of these and other points see Mendis and Muellbauer (1984). See also *National Institute Economic Review*, no. 101, August 1982, which contains a series of papers on Britain's comparative productivity, and Daly *et al.* (1985).

manner in which the traditional relationship between the commercial banks and their prime lenders is changing, and the role the industrial economist has to play in assisting commercial banks in this changing environment.

7.2 Securitisation

One of the most fundamental changes now taking place in the world's major financial markets is the process of what has become known as securitisation. Whilst the concept of securitisation is relatively simple its effects are far reaching. Securitisation is the generic term applied to the process by which financing takes place through the issue of tradeable notes or paper. Debt which had become securitised is thus, in theory at least, more liquid in so far as it may be traded in the market.

The movement towards securitisation has been driven by a number of factors, not the least of which is cost. The largest multinational companies found that they were able to achieve at least as high a credit rating as their banks, and correspondingly raise funds more cheaply. In such circumstances, corporate treasurers are clearly not going to call upon their commercial bank for funds in the traditional way. The position of the banks was made worse by the difficulties they experienced in their lending to a number of sovereign borrowers. The banks, having lent large sums to the developing nations, found that a significant proportion of their assets were immobilised and their credit rating suffered accordingly. Increasingly, therefore, major companies have sought to raise funds through the issue of Eurobonds or Euronotes.

Alongside cost, a number of other factors have assisted the development of marketable debt. Geographical shifts in international capital flows in the 1980s have seen a diminution of the OPEC surplus and the emergence of a sustained and growing Japanese balance-of-payments surplus. Compared to the 1970s, when petro-dollars were mainly recycled in the form of commercial bank loans (OPEC's clearly preferred form of investment was bank deposits), the Japanese have preferred to invest in securitised debt. At the same time, the deregulation and liberalisation of the world's major financial markets have meant ever-increasing competition between financial institutions to develop new forms of financial instruments and services. The development of information technology has further broken down the barriers between international and national markets and intensified this process. To illustrate the magnitude of these changes, the Group of Ten central banks reported that the arrangement of syndicated loans fell from

$100 billion in 1981 to $20 billion in 1985, while issues of international bonds and floating-rate notes rose from $40 billion to $160 billion.[2]

The ability of financial institutions to develop new products may be witnessed by the differing forms marketable debt may take. Debt, for example, can be issued with a fixed interest rate or with a floating rate. Similarly, currency and interest rate swaps have proved increasingly popular. Marks and Spencer, for example, having achieved a 'Triple A' rating from Standard and Poor and from Moody, raised $150m in the Eurobond market. It then proceeded to swap the dollar proceeds of this issue for sterling funds at a floating rate of interest marginally below London interbank rates. By such means, a company and its financial advisers are able to decide in which markets conditions are most favourable for fund raising and to exploit any inefficiencies in market pricing.

In these circumstances, the role of the commercial bank and its relationship with major corporate customers requires some revision. No longer is a major corporate customer likely to ask its bank to extend lines of credit in the traditional mode, but it will rather seek advice and assistance in the issue of its own marketable debt. Profitable opportunities for a major financial institution in these circumstances lie in earning fees by arranging a bond or note issue, underwriting and/or providing standby facilities. Many institutions have considerable placing power in the markets, and this can be a key ingredient in the success of an issue. Agency work offers relatively healthy returns when compared to some of the lending which took place in the 1970s, much of which was to the Third World and proved to be not very profitable.

These developments in the financial markets have not only been to the benefit of companies but have been actively encouraged by the banks. As a result of their substantial lending to the developing nations during the 1970s, the banks found that their capital resources had by the early 1980s become over-stretched. Given the emphasis placed by their banking supervisors on strengthening their capital ratios, the banks were encouraged to meet their customers' demands for credit in ways that avoided disclosure on their own balance sheet. The provision of standby facilities has proved to be one popular method of engineering off-balance sheet financing, although the subsequent growth of these arrangements has made banking supervisors uneasy. In the UK, the Bank of England has been particularly concerned about the long-term risk associated with the obligations financial institutions have assumed in respect of note issuance facilities. Discussion has focussed on the

2   See Bank of England (1986a). This note summarises the detailed report prepared by the study group established by the Group of Ten central banks and published by the Bank for International Settlements (1986).

circumstances in which, the financial position of the borrower having deteriorated, the bank would be called upon to honour the standby facility granted to allow the original issue of marketable debt. As a result, the Bank of England has considered that it is necessary for these obligations to be taken into account when measuring a bank's capital adequacy. These obligations, as a provisional measure, are to be treated as contingent liabilities for capital adequacy purposes and included at a weight of 0.5 in the calculation of the risk-asset ratio, whether or not the facility has been drawn down by the borrower.[3]

The recognition that standby facilities, if utilised, could place banks in a position of some difficulty has also led the Bank of England to suggest that the banks include standby facilities within their existing credit limit for individual borrowers. Consequently, before the granting of such facilities, a full credit assessment of the borrower should be undertaken (Bank of England, 1985a, p. 248).

The Bank of England's actions reflect the difficulty of assessing the risks involved with securitisation and the need for the banks to adopt prudent practice when undertaking these new forms of lending. Certainly, the strength of the secondary markets has yet to be fully tested, and the decline in interest rates over the last two years has undoubtedly helped to make tradeable debt attractive. More recently, the floating rate note market experienced a loss of liquidity with respect to perpetual issues, where a reassessment of their value against other tradeable paper took place. Paradoxically, perpetual notes have in the main been issued by commercial banks to enhance their capital base.

In an attempt to anticipate and to be responsive to the changes taking place in these markets, the commercial banks have orientated their business policies accordingly. The Midland Bank, for example, is being organised into three major sectors: UK banking, global banking and investment banking. The work of those economists analysing industrial structure within the Bank will be primarily to service the needs of the UK and global banking sectors.

Whilst securitisation will enable the largest corporates to issue marketable debt, not all companies will have sufficient standing in the market to raise the funds they need, and these will continue to seek lines of credit from the commercial banks. The danger for banks is that, given the loss of their largest and generally less risky corporate borrowers, the quality of the banks' portfolio of lending could well deteriorate, as they lend to second-tier and smaller companies that are unable to gain access to the securities market at reasonable cost.

---

[3]   The notice to recognised banks and licensed deposit-takers was issued by the Bank of England, Banking Supervision Division on the 3 April 1985. For details see Bank of England, 1985a, pp. 248-9.

7.3 Industry risk

The Bank of England has recently issued a consultative paper on the Bank's policy towards large exposures. It states that

> . . . large exposures give[n] rise to supervisory concern because of the risk that an excessive exposure to an individual counterparty, a group of associated counterparts or a country or economic sector could, if it proved to be irrevocable, threaten the solvency of the lending bank (Bank of England, 1986c, p. 1).

This latest concern with the degree of concentration of risk associated in lending follows experiences in the United States and in the UK. In the US, where many of the developments in banking and corporate finance have preceded the changes taking place in the UK, there is evidence that the American banks have had to write-off substantial sums against their industrial loans in recent years. In 1984, write-offs reached a record $1.9bn, even though the US economy was in a period of recovery, when historically corporate failure tends to be less (Hindle, 1986). Although some proportion of the write-offs might be attributed to the nature of the recovery, the majority of the remainder have been blamed on the impact of securitisation, leading to a worsening in the quality of the banks' portfolios. Over 50 per cent of these loans were concentrated in three industrial categories: energy; construction, mining and farm machinery; and wholesaling and retailing. In other words, some industries were substantially more risky to fund than others.

More recent evidence from the United States is provided by the experience of Texan banks which, having lent considerable sums to the energy and farming sectors, have found to their cost the difficulties created by over-exposure to economic sectors noted for their volatility. Johnson Matthey Bankers (JMB) similarly provides a clear example of a financial institution in the UK committing too much cash to too few customers. The recognition that lending to different industries entails different degrees of risk, and that lending to a number of companies in a single industry leads to a cumulative risk, brings to the forefront the analysis of industry risk.

In the UK it has been clearly recognised that for a bank to be over-exposed in a particular economic sector is potentially harmful. Under current arrangements, UK banks are required to provide the Bank of England each month with a breakdown of their lending and acceptances to UK residents based upon the Bank's industrial classification. On the basis of this information the Bank of England is able to monitor the banks' exposures, and to ensure that as far as industrial concentration is concerned a bank's lending policies are prudent.

On the basis of the above discussion, banks are developing their ability to analyse industry risk to parallel the sophisticated credit techniques they use in their other principal areas of business. In the personal lending market, for example, banks are able to credit-rate individuals, whilst in more recent years they have developed country risk techniques to credit-rate countries. The importance of industrial structure has also been recognised with respect to lending to the corporate customer. The recognition that companies operate in an environment which is a complex amalgam of economic, technological, social and political factors is moving the vetting of corporate lending requests away from traditional credit techniques which have relied solely on such factors as the assessment of security, management accounts and personal attributes. Similarly, although financial ratios derived from accounting data can be of assistance in this area, there are some well-known difficulties associated with this technique. Further, as accounting data do not fully capture the economic environment in which the company is operating, the importance of industry analysis remains undiminished.

The importance of industrial structure has indeed been recognised by the major credit-rating agencies in the US, which are now actively seeking to set up branches in London, anticipating the need for their services in the wake of the recent changes in the financial markets. Standard and Poor, one of the two major US companies, includes industry risk and market position, alongside the use of more traditional financial ratios, together with an evaluation of the company's management, when assessing major corporates.

7.4 The role of the industrial economist

From the preceding discussion, it should be clear that analysis of industrial structure has an important, and increasing, role to play in helping a bank determine its lending portfolio, and in identifying risks and opportunities. Whilst macroeconomic models may be useful in providing insights into the operation of the economy at an aggregate level, their lack of sophistication in analysing the performance of individual sectors of the economy makes their use limited for the work being discussed. Disaggregated models, such as the model constructed by the Cambridge Growth Project (CGP), do however provide forecasts at the level of individual industries. The model is suited to analysing and forecasting structural change, given that developments at the level of individual industries collectively determine the movement of aggregate variables. Such models provide a useful and detailed framework against which the individual economist can compare and contrast his own data and analysis. The provision of forecasts broken down by industries in line with the Standard Industrial Classification, and with the additional benefit of regional forecasts, can assist in the banks' optimal allocation of resources, both in terms of manpower and financial services.

It may be helpful at this point to discuss the differing requirements of the stock market analyst working for a broker, and of the industrial economist advising a commercial bank. The equity analyst primarily takes a short-term view, relying strongly on traditional stock market information and official economic indicators (e.g. consumers' expenditure, retail sales, indices of production etc). Analysts will generally consider the performance of the major companies operating in the industry, presenting information on the company's marketing and business strategies alongside its recent stock market performance. Qualitative information on a company is likely to have been built up by contacts with the industry and by thorough desk research. Most brokers do not, however, have sophisticated models of individual industry sectors, although many do have macro-models forecasting the overall performance of the economy. Forecasts of a company's next set of profit figures is likely to be based upon a process of extrapolation, allied to informed judgement on the company's progress. Compared to the analyst, the bank economist is much more concerned with the longer-term performance of the industry. Over this longer time period, the approach adopted by the CGP has significant advantages over the methods used by the analysts whose outlook is very short-term and biased to the performance of the stock market.

Looking in detail at the work undertaken, the use of industrial analysis as a tool in decision-making may take place at three levels within the organisation. Firstly, analysis of industrial structure forms a significant input into a bank's strategic planning, assisting in the analysis of its portfolio spread. The distribution of risk across and between industries can be considered in the light of projected industrial performance, and decisions made to increase or decrease exposure by industrial sector. For the UK, research has shown that Britain has a relatively weak presence in the research-intensive industries, which are generally projected to demonstrate the fastest rates of growth (see Smith, 1986). The location of these industries across the regions is also one factor to consider when analysing regional performance.

The second level at which industry analysis is able to provide a significant input into the bank's decision-making is in the development of in-depth industry studies. Analysis of the performance of individual sectors provides the backdrop against which lending decisions can be made. These may range from the provision of traditional forms of credit, or the provision of standby facilities, to the financing of management buy-outs which have been increasingly popular in recent years. Against an overall assessment of the industry structure, conduct and performance, company-specific information can enable the comparative performance of potential client companies to be undertaken. Assessment of a company's competitive position, and whether it has achieved a competitive advantage, is crucial. Even though a company is located in a growing industry this does not automatically mean that it will prosper. Similarly, well-run companies in declining sectors may perform very well.

In conducting company analysis, the various commercial on-line company data bases provide an easy and readily available means of obtaining the latest company information, and for constructing industry groups. Having produced a report on a selected industry, subsequent up-dating at frequent intervals allows senior management to have a clear framework against which they can review the performance of the industry for which they are responsible, and the companies with which they have specific relationships.

Finally, reviewing its portfolio in the light of industry forecasts will enable the bank to identify areas for further development. Having identified the industries where the bank's presence is below the level desired, marketing efforts may be concentrated and senior executives assigned target companies in an industry. Since the time of senior executives is very expensive, and a scarce resource for the organisation, an exercise in targeting can be highly cost-effective.

7.5 Summary

The preceding analysis has, I hope, quite clearly demonstrated the increasing complexity of the relationship between corporate customer and commercial bank. The speed of financial innovation provides an ever-increasing challenge in a highly competitive market. To be able to identify clearly the risks of providing finance both through on- and off-balance-sheet financing, appraisal of the environment in which a firm operates is of great significance. The importance of industrial structure means that a disaggregated approach to modelling the economy is of major benefit and assists the industrial economist in advising senior management in their business decision-making. It is anticipated that as the tools of analysis grow ever more powerful, and the importance of industrial and commercial information continues to grow, the demands on the services of economists engaged in the analysis of markets and industries will increase further.

8

DEVELOPMENTS IN THE UK'S INTERNATIONAL TRADING PERFORMANCE

Andrew Kilpatrick and Christopher Moir[*]

8.1 Introduction

The achievement and maintenance of balance-of-payments equilibrium without sacrificing control over macroeconomic policy instruments has long remained a goal of British economic policy. More often than not, major restrictions on domestic policy have had to be imposed to compensate for the economy's tendency towards balance-of-payments disequilibrium on the current account. In the 1960s this tendency resulted in a succession of fiscal policy tightenings designed to squeeze domestic demand and its associated slippage into imports. In the 1970s, under a regime of floating exchange rates, the same tendency resulted in a depreciating exchange rate which put upward pressure on the inflation rate. Again the consequence was fiscal and/or monetary policy tightening to restore equilibrium.

The tendency towards disequilibrium in the balance of payments has meant that the overall rate of growth of the economy has been constrained and this in turn has implied a slower growth of employment than might otherwise have prevailed. A key problem throughout, which domestic macroeconomic policy *per se* could do little to influence under either exchange rate regime, has been the failure of UK suppliers to meet the growing needs of domestic and foreign consumers at an adequate rate. Improvement in trade performance is thus an essential ingredient of any strategy to raise the trend rate of growth of UK output

[*] The views expressed in this chapter are those of the individual authors and do not necessarily coincide with those of the National Economic Development Office or any of the committees associated with it.

141

and employment.

The arrival of North Sea oil, which coincided with a period of high real oil prices, transformed the UK balance of payments. Instead of a chronic tendency towards deficit, the substantial windfall gain of oil revenues led to sustained current account surpluses from 1980 onwards, with a peak surplus amounting to 2.4 per cent of GDP being recorded in 1981. This was also achieved despite the major appreciation of the sterling real exchange rate which occurred between 1978 and 1980. Since 1981 non-oil GDP growth has been strong and has been sustained longer than in earlier growth-spurt periods, helped in part because the current account has not moved into deficit.

Despite the massive turnround in the UK balance-of-payments position during the early 1980s, many commentators have felt uneasy with the position, frequently arguing that North Sea oil revenue has masked underlying difficulties. For many UK manufacturers and producers of traded services there has been no mask at all, since the upward movement in the sterling exchange rate squeezed export margins and encouraged import competition further; and this occurred on top of an already strong adverse trend in trade performance. Together with the downturn in real domestic demand in 1980-81, the combination of events put a major squeeze on the traded goods sector, with the result that many more companies ceased to trade than might have been expected.

Notwithstanding the importance of the oil sector and the shift to services of various kinds, one consequence of this deflationary period was an absolute shrinkage in the capacity of the UK manufacturing sector, with some sectors faring much worse than others. There was probably also a restriction on the rate of expansion of many service industries. The exact size of the change in the productive capacity of the UK is uncertain, being complicated by the absence of adequate information on capital stocks (particularly on the rate of scrapping which was especially rapid in the early part of this decade), but few authors dispute the proposition that a reduction in manufacturing capacity did occur between 1980 and 1985. More recent events may have led to the creation of new capacity, particularly in some services, and more generally to a better rate of utilisation of the remaining capital stock. Nonetheless, if the traded goods and services sectors are ultimately to replace the output and income provided by oil, more may be required of investment, not only in plant and equipment but also in R&D, marketing, and training. Other influences on non-price competitiveness, such as delivery and quality, will also require continuing improvement.

The Select Committee Report on Overseas Trade by Lord Aldington in 1985 noted many of the failings of UK manufacturing industry's trade performance, and urged that steps be taken to strengthen the manufacturing base to provide a competitive capability which would outlast North Sea oil and which would also satisfy the UK consumer's predilection for foreign goods. One of the major premises of this Report was the probable run-down of production of North Sea oil, the peak of which was expected to occur around 1985, and the re-emergence of a deficit on oil around 1990. It was this that gave rise to the Committee's conclusion that

> unless the climate is changed so that steps can be taken to enlarge the manufacturing base, combat import penetration, and stimulate the export of manufactured goods, as oil revenues diminish the country will experience adverse effects which taken together, constitute a grave threat to the standard of living and to the economic and political stability of the nation (para. 231.6).

Such an alarming conclusion has naturally not found favour in all quarters (see, for instance, the government's reply to the House of Lords Report, Department of Trade and Industry (1985)) but concern over the balance of payments has begun to re-emerge more widely during the last year, not only because of this Report and its implications but also because of the rapid and large drop in oil prices. These have fallen from roughly $28 per barrel in 1985 to $18 per barrel in early 1987 and this has therefore approximately halved the revenue from North Sea oil within one year instead of the four years envisaged by the Aldington Committee. The fact that the UK has managed so far to withstand this change without a major foreign exchange crisis is perhaps some measure of the degree to which the House of Lords Report over-dramatised the UK's predicament, and the government's supporters have not been slow in making this point. Nonetheless, the longer-term implications of the drop in oil revenue on the balance of payments need examination and this chapter aims to contribute to this by looking at the trade picture in detail.

The initial adjustment to the UK's lower oil wealth has been made through the depreciation of sterling, but on this occasion the traditional counterpart to such an adjustment (*viz.* deflationary policy) has been absent because of the direct beneficial effects of lower oil prices on inflation. To this extent the initial adjustment was smoother than might have been expected and did not dent the credibility of the government's pledge to control inflation. Whether it can be assumed that there will not be a further depreciation of sterling with adverse inflationary consequences is debatable. Foreign exchange markets' expectations are notoriously fickle and it may prove more difficult to convince foreign investors of the worth of the UK economy once the full effects of the lower oil revenues come to be felt on the balance of payments. Already preliminary figures suggest the current account for 1986 will be in deficit, while the latest available forecasts for 1987 indicate a significant expected worsening of the position (Table 8.1).

Table 8.1   *The UK balance-of-payments current account, 1980-87*

	£bn			
1980	2.9			
1981	6.2			
1982	3.9			
1983	3.1			
1984	1.2			
1985	3.6			
1986 Est	-1.1			
Forecast	HM Treasury[a]	NIESR[b]	LBS[b]	Liverpool[c]
1987	-2.5	-2.6	-2.3	-2.6

Notes: [a] Financial Statement and Budget Report 1987.
         [b] February 1987.
         [c] December 1986.
Sources: CSO, DTI, model groups.

A short-run deficit on the current account at the level indicated by the above forecasts might be sustainable without serious adverse effects on growth. For the longer-term position to be secure much depends on invisibles and the reaction of industry to the improvement in competitiveness and the reversal of the adverse underlying trends in UK trade performance that have dominated for so long.

8.2 The overall balance-of-payments picture

A key question is whether the expected deterioration in the UK's current account is likely to be a temporary phenomenon, as the economy adjusts to lower oil revenues, or more permanent. Naturally there is great uncertainty over the future price of oil and, with the UK likely to continue as a major producer for some time, the balance-of-payments picture is somewhat complicated. Nonetheless, most commentators and oil industry analysts appear unwilling to predict a return to the high real oil prices of the early 1980s, for a period of perhaps up to ten years. Even if there was a resurgence of oil prices in five to ten years, after a period of oil prices at $20 per barrel, the real contribution of oil to the balance of payments would be considerably lower than at its peak in 1985. This is because the production of North Sea oil would be considerably less, perhaps between 1/3 and 2/3 of the peak level (see Bank of England, 1986b). In the absence of a likely turnround in oil prices, therefore, there is merit in considering the composition of trade and the implications of the 'reverse oil price shock' for the future performance of manufacturing and service industries.

The current account may be divided into five main components: oil; non-oil commodities; services; interest, profits and dividends; and transfers. Since non-oil commodities form the greater part of trade, it is worthwhile to sub-divide this category into a further five components: food, drink and tobacco; basic materials; semi-manufactures; finished manufactures; and other commodities. Table 8.2 shows the trade balances on this basis for four periods which are broadly comparable in terms of the economic cycle: one pre-first oil crisis, 1971-2; 1977-8; 1984-5; and the latest information for 1986. Because of the problems caused by short-term fluctuations, two-year averages have been used. The effect of inflation has been stripped out by use of the GDP deflator. Although this is not an ideal procedure, it is sufficient to illustrate the main developments.

Taking the periods 1971-2 and 1977-8 first, it is apparent that the worsening of the oil account was balanced by improvements in services, even after allowance is made for what appears to have been an exceptionally successful period on the travel account. It is interesting to note that the balance of trade on manufactures deteriorated only slightly between these two dates. There is also a deterioration in the transfers account. This item is largely government transfers and the change can be explained by the increase in UK contributions (principally customs duties and VAT) to the European Community following membership in 1973.

Moving on to the 1984-5 period, the comparison shows clearly the impact of North Sea oil. The oil account is substantially improved, a turnround of the order of £7-8bn as compared with the pre-North Sea oil position. Perhaps rather surprisingly given the adverse exchange rate movement and the associated deterioration in competitiveness, improvements also occurred in food, drink and tobacco (+£2bn) and basic materials (+£0.5bn to £2bn), as well as increased interest, profits

Table 8.2   *UK balance-of-payments current account at constant 1980 prices: selected periods (£m)*

Annual averages	1971-2	1977-8	1984-5	1986
Goods				
Oil and other fuels	-2305	-3575	4442	1932
Food, drink and tobacco	-4705	-4403	-2631	-2645
Basic materials	-2646	-3345	-2027	-1583
Semi-manufactures	1851	2133	-22	-550
Finished manufactures	6529	5782	-2528	-3495
Other commodities	370	645	365	636
Total non-oil commodities	1399	812	-6843	-7636
Total visible trade	-906	-2763	-2401	-5704
Services				
General government services	-1081	-1036	-912	-946
Sea transport	-227	55	-847	-848
Civil aviation	198	360	223	-149
Travel	162	1535	194	-372
Financial and other services	2838	3795	4875	5991
Total services	1890	4709	3533	3676
Interest, profits and dividends	1864	764	2795	2941
Transfers	-760	-2110	-2146	-1673
Current account	2088	598	1780	-760

and dividends (+£1bn to £2bn); but the decline of sea transport is also apparent (-£0.5 to -£1bn). The current account is brought into line by a significant deterioration of the manufacturing trade balance which falls by between £10bn and £11bn, to which the decline in finished manufactures makes the largest contribution, around £8bn to £9bn.

The comparison of 1986 and 1984-5 is instructive, for while it is clear that many balances are unchanged in real terms, this is not true for the oil surplus which is more than halved (giving a deterioration of around £2.5 bn) nor is it true for the manufactures balance which continues to worsen by a further £1bn. Some compensation is found in increased financial and other services earnings, and in interests, profits and dividends revenues and a reduced net contribution to the European Community budget.

Table 8.3 summarises the changes in the balance of payments between 1971-2 and 1986, expressed at constant 1980 prices. The period as a whole is characterised by major improvements in the oil account and in financial and other services, together with gains in food, drink and tobacco, and in interest, profits and dividends. Against this is set the

Table 8.3   *Major changes in the UK current account between 1971-2 and 1986 at constant 1980 prices (£bn)*

	Change in balance (approximately)
Oil and other fuels	+ 4
Food, drink and tobacco	+ 2
Basic materials	+ 1
Manufactures	- 12.5
Financial and other services	+ 3
Interest, profits and dividends	+ 1
European Community	- 1

massive deterioration in the manufacturing trade balance.

The performance in net manufacturing trade is so manifestly poor that it merits a more detailed investigation. Before turning to this, however, it is worth considering briefly to what extent any of the changes shown in Table 8.2 are one-off movements rather than trends that may be expected to continue to a greater or lesser degree. In view of the earlier comment on oil prices and production, it would seem reasonable not to anticipate much advance on the oil surplus recorded in 1986. Elsewhere the picture is less clear, although Table 8.2 suggests that perhaps the improvement in the food, drink and tobacco account was a step change. It is also the case that the improvement in basic materials has occurred partly as a result of weakening commodity prices which behave in a cyclical fashion. Any further deterioration in manufactures therefore has to be matched by advances in financial services and so on. The scale of the problem, were the position of manufacturing to continue to worsen, is illustrated in Table 8.4 where the relative contributions of manufacturing exports and financial service credits to foreign income derived from exports of goods and services as a whole are shown.

The table shows that the share of export earnings contributed by manufacturing has declined in the last decade while that of financial services has increased. Manufacturing, however, still produces about 4.5 times as much income as services. In other words, for each percentage point decline in the growth of manufacturing exports (or rise in imports) the financial and other services sectors would have to grow some 4.5 per cent faster (either by higher exports or lower imports or both) to preserve equilibrium. Even though exports of financial and other services grew by 4.3 per cent p.a. during this decade, faster than the 2.7 per cent p.a. recorded by exports of manufactures, it has not been sufficiently fast to give confidence that the UK can necessarily rely on

Table 8.4 *The contribution of manufacturing exports and financial services to foreign earnings from trade in goods and services, 1975 and 1985*

	Percentage of all credits from exports of goods and services	
	1975	1985
Semi-manufactures	21.7	19.6
Finished manufactures	37.0	31.5
Total manufactures	58.6	51.1
Financial and other services	10.7	11.6
Other (incl. oil)	30.7	37.3
Total	100.0	100.0

services to fill the trade gap left by the fall in performance of traded manufactured goods; the latter are still important.

One other major contributor to the balance of payments, interest, profits and dividends, has developed considerably and its effects cannot be completely ignored in this context. In terms of total earnings, interest, profits and dividends credits in 1985 contributed in total almost as much as manufactures. There are, however, many problems with measurement and valuation here. The data are subject to major revisions, partly because it is difficult to associate the income with any particular industry, and because of the problems in monitoring the marked daily fluctuations in capital flows into and out of the UK. Such volatility feeds through into the credits and debits on interest, profits and dividends and makes their future contribution to the balance of payments very uncertain. A full interpretation of this and its implications for the balance of payments is properly the subject of another paper and is not dealt with here. Despite their major contribution to the current account, the inherent volatility of interest, profits and dividend flows suggests it is unlikely the UK could rely on a 'rentier' role and maintain adequate economic growth. Notwithstanding this qualification, the focus of this chapter is on the behaviour of trade in manufactures and we now turn to this in more detail.

8.3 Trade in manufactures

The behaviour of the balance of trade in manufactures during the 1970s and 1980s has been in marked contrast to that of earlier decades. In the fourteen years between 1958 and 1972 there was virtually no deterioration in the manufactures trade balance, although the UK did of course lose a share of world trade. More recently, over the same length of time, 1972 to 1986, this share has not only continued to fall but in addition the manufacturing trade position has worsened by some £8bn.

In examining this performance it is useful to separate finished manufactures into three components: consumer goods, intermediate goods, and capital goods. Since some elements of trade are volatile (e.g. ships, aircraft, precious stones) and can distort the underlying picture, they are excluded in the discussion below. The figures in this section of the paper are based on volume movements, expressed at constant 1980 unit values.

Figure 8.1   *UK exports and imports of consumer goods in volume terms (based on 1980 unit values), 1970-86*

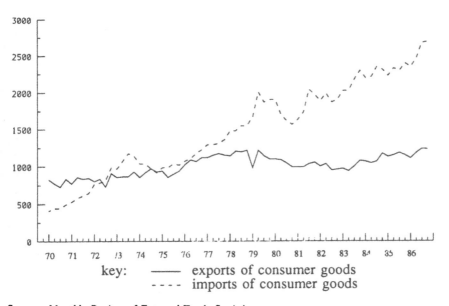

key: ——— exports of consumer goods
         - - - - imports of consumer goods

Source: *Monthly Review of External Trade Statistics.*

Figs 8.1 to 8.4 show the behaviour on a quarterly basis of exports and imports for the three groups of finished manufactures together with that for semi-manufactures for the period since 1970. The gap between the export and import lines represents the balance of trade at constant

Figure 8.2 *UK exports and imports of capital goods in volume terms (based on 1980 unit values), 1970-86*

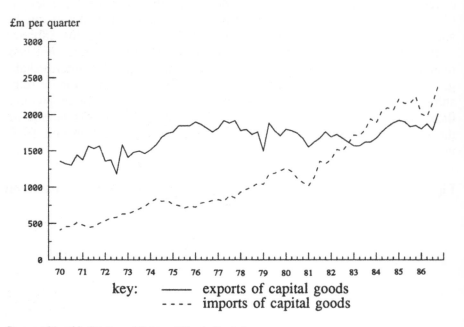

£m per quarter

key: ———— exports of capital goods
        - - - - imports of capital goods

Source: *Monthly Review of External Trade Statistics.*

prices. It can readily be seen that the trade balances of all three groups of finished manufactures deteriorate throughout. The same is true of semi-manufactures, although to a less significant degree. It is also noticeable that the trends appear fairly smooth, particularly imports, despite the turbulent economic period which these data cover. Whereas, in the early 1970s, the UK was a net exporter of each group of goods, by 1986 this only remained true of intermediate goods and even here it remained true only by a very narrow margin. Since the performance of semi-manufactures does not contribute substantially to the explanation of the deterioration of the manufacturing trade balance as a whole it is not considered further.

8.4 Consumer and capital goods trade

Figs 8.1-8.4 show that, while a deterioration in performance occurs in all three groups, consumer goods moves into deficit first. By 1972, the

Figure 8.3   *UK exports and imports of finished intermediate manufactures in volume terms (based on 1980 unit values),
1970-86*

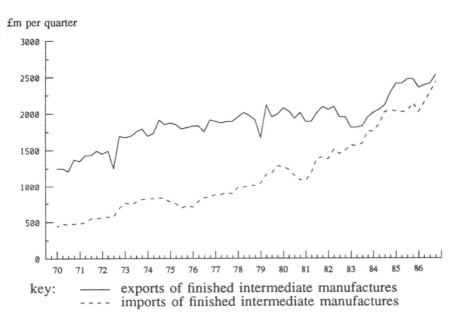

key: ——— exports of finished intermediate manufactures
          - - - - imports of finished intermediate manufactures

Source: *Monthly Review of External Trade Statistics.*

UK was purchasing more consumer goods from abroad than it sold
overseas and this has remained the case continuously from 1975. In the
case of capital goods, however, the move into deficit is later, in 1982,
while intermediate goods, as noted above, have not yet quite reached the
deficit stage.

The poor performance on the consumer goods front is well-known
and since it is largely due to a major shift in trade in passenger cars the
consequences are evident daily. Nonetheless, it is important to note that
the trade balances of both capital goods and intermediate finished
manufactures have also deteriorated to a considerable extent and, when
taken together, by more than that of consumer goods. The data show
that capital goods have performed particularly badly, almost matching
(with a lag) the worsening position of consumer goods. This has been
especially so since the mid 1970s. Over the period 1977-86 the capital
goods trade balance in constant price terms fell by £5.3bn as compared
with a £4.8bn deterioration in consumer goods.

Figure 8.4   *UK exports and imports of semi-manufactures in volume terms (based on 1980 unit values), 1970-86*

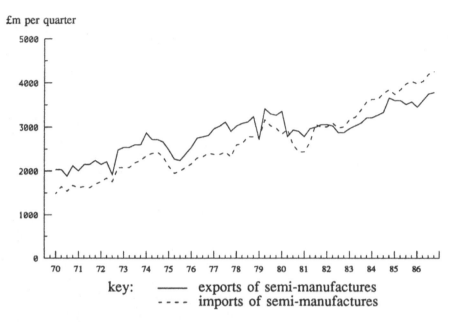

£m per quarter

key: ——— exports of semi-manufactures
              - - - - imports of semi-manufactures

Source: *Monthly Review of External Trade Statistics.*

8.5 Trade performance

An alternative presentation of trade performance is provided by the measure $(X-M)/(X+M)$ where X = exports and M = imports. The advantage of using this statistic is that it makes allowance for the effect of the growth in trade volumes on trade balances. Simply measuring the trade balance, $X-M$, without allowing for the growth of trade, may result in the impression that competitiveness has declined when in fact it has not. A fall in the $(X-M)/(X+M)$ measure indicates unambiguously that relative performance has deteriorated (see Singh, 1979). The characteristic of this measure is that it varies from +1, representing full UK comparative advantage, to -1, where all trade is in imports. It is straightforward to show that, for given constant rates of growth of exports and imports with, say, imports growth exceeding that of exports, the path of this variable is a logistic shape sloping downwards from left to right. The steepness of the slope depends simply on the difference between import and export growth.

Figure 8.5 *Competitive performance in consumer goods, 1970-86*

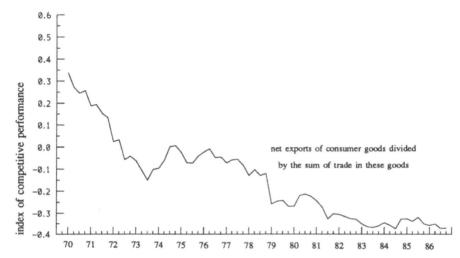

Source: Derived from *Monthly Review of External Trade Statistics.*

Figure 8.6 *Competitive performance in capital goods, 1970-86*

Source: Derived from *Monthly Review of External Trade Statistics.*

Figs 8.5-8.7 show the pattern of this variable for consumer goods, capital goods and intermediate goods over the same period as before.

Figure 8.7   *Competitive performance in finished intermediate manufactures, 1970-86*

net exports of finished intermediate goods
divided by the sum of trade in these goods

Source: Derived from *Monthly Review of External Trade Statistics*.

Recalling that this measure only declines when the UK share of world trade for the relevant commodity group falls back, it can be seen that in each case UK competitiveness has weakened. As with the balance of trade the worst performance over the whole period is recorded by consumer goods, although since the mid 1970s the deterioration in capital goods has outpaced that of consumer goods.

Before turning to the behaviour of capital goods in detail, it is worth noting the distinctive gradual flattening of the consumer goods 'competitive' path as illustrated in Fig. 8.5. This is consistent with the path that may be expected when import growth consistently exceeds export growth over a long period. There are possible indications that a similar pattern may have emerged in capital goods in the last few years (Fig. 8.6). In the case of consumer goods this development is explained by the behaviour of imports, since export growth has varied considerably less. The marked flattening out of the consumer goods charts suggest, on the basis of a simple extrapolation, that the worst of the deteriorating competitive position of the UK in this sector may be over. Nonetheless, because of the substantially higher deficit in consumer goods trade that now prevails, it is not obvious that this entails a slower absolute rise in the deficit than previously. If the index remained at -0.4, it would imply a widening trade deficit at a rate equal to the sum of import and export increases multiplied by 0.4. On recent

Figure 8.8   *Unit labour costs in manufacturing*

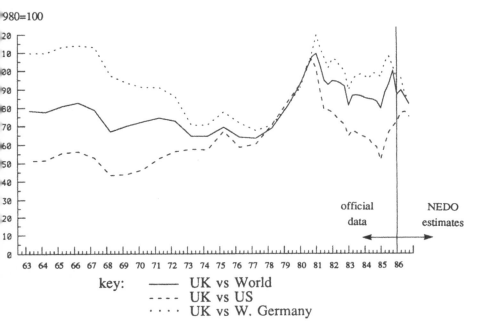

key: —— UK vs World
       - - - - UK vs US
       · · · · UK vs W. Germany

Source: DTI, *Monthly Review of External Trade Statistics.*

trends this would represent a worsening of around £300m p.a. expressed at constant 1980 unit values - less than the average £420 p.a. deterioration actually recorded over the period as a whole.

   The extrapolation of the observed trends in consumer goods above suggests less cause for pessimism than perhaps some predictions, especially those which are based on models which make insufficient allowance for the non-linear relationship indicated. (For a recent discussion of non-linear relationships in import modelling, see Gleed, 1986.) There may indeed be good reason to be less pessimistic about the consumer goods trade balance, since the trend depicted above reflects a growing degree of import 'saturation'. In many consumer goods sectors import penetration is already complete with, in some cases, virtually no domestic productive capability left. In passenger cars, for example, penetration of the domestic market by foreign car producers rose very rapidly during the late 1960s and 1970s, while UK producers struggled unsuccessfully to expand overseas sales at the same rate. In recent times the pace of import growth has slowed down, as ultimately it must, because its growth has become increasingly limited by the rate of expansion of the domestic market which in turn is dependent on the overall rate of growth of the whole economy. In the UK this growth rate is considerably below the pace of import change that characterised the 1970s.

A further determinant of import growth which applies in the case of cars, and in a number of other consumer goods sectors as well, lies in the extent to which inward investment and the associated production has replaced imports. In the case of cars, which are dominated by a number of multinational companies, this behaviour has exerted a major influence on the pattern of UK trade. In recent years there has been a substantial degree of inward investment in motor vehicles, for example, by Ford at Dagenham and Nissan in Washington, which supports UK export performance in the absence of a major domestically-owned producer (BL and Rover are tiny in world terms) but also helps to some extent to explain the reduction in the rate of import growth. It is possible, if for instance the UK were used as a major launching base by some companies trying to expand in the European market, that export growth might increase. On this basis, the prospects for the balance of trade in consumer goods in the medium term are perhaps brighter than they first appear.

Fig. 8.6 depicts the performance of the capital goods group using the same measure as above. As with consumer goods the trend is downwards, indicating a decline in competitive position. Unlike consumer goods, however, there is no pronounced flattening of the picture throughout the period, although the chart is noticeably flatter from 1983 onwards. The picture for intermediate goods (Fig. 8.7) shows a steady decline in competitiveness although at a less rapid rate than for either of the other two categories.

The position on capital goods taken together with intermediate goods, many of which are parts of capital equipment (for example, electric motors and microprocessors) and cannot be easily distinguished from capital goods themselves, looks problematic. First, the competitive position has deteriorated sharply since 1978 and, although this decline has slowed down for capital goods in the last few years, the rapid growth of trade volumes means that the deficit is increasing fast even with a constant $(X-M)/(X+M)$ ratio. The trend decline in these groups implies an average deterioration of around £400m p.a. Second, Figs 8.2 and 8.3 show that imports of these products accelerated rapidly from 1981 and that the very rapid growth between 1981 and 1984 coincides with a period when domestic fixed investment in plant and machinery was relatively flat. The capital goods picture is the next area of investigation but before moving on to this it is worth recapitulating.

Table 8.5   *Average annual growth rates of export and import volumes in manufacturing and its sub-groups: 1970-74, 1974-80, 1980-86III (% p.a.)*

	1970-1974	1974-1980	1980-1986III
Export volume			
All manufactured exports[a]	6.7	1.6	2.4
of which			
consumer goods	3.8	2.3	1.7
capital goods	4.6	1.1	0.7
intermediate finished goods	8.8	1.9	3.1
semi-manufactures	7.7	1.4	3.2
Import volume			
All manufactured imports[a]	13.1	5.0	8.2
of which			
consumer goods	19.9	9.1	6.6
capital goods	14.3	6.0	10.3
intermediate finished goods	14.2	6.2	10.4
semi-manufactures	10.0	2.2	7.1

Note: [a] Excluding erratics.
Source: *Monthly Review of External Trade Statistics.*

Table 8.5 summarises the picture so far. It shows average annual growth rates of export and import volumes for manufactures and the sub-groups we have been discussing for three periods, 1970-74, 1974-80 and 1980-86. A number of points in addition to those already discussed may be made. First, in no period and for no category does export volume growth exceed import volume growth. Second, the rapid expansion of trade in the early period has not been matched subsequently, but growth in 1980-86 has been faster than in the mid 1970s. It is interesting to note that import growth has moved back closer to the earlier rapid rate than has export growth. This can be seen particularly clearly in capital and intermediate goods. Third, the slowdown in consumer goods import growth is illustrated but it is noticeable that the same pattern emerges in consumer goods exports, although to a much less marked degree. Fourth, while imports of all other categories have accelerated since the 1974-80 period, so too have exports with the exception of capital goods. Here, the average rate of growth was 0.7 per cent p.a. in the 1980-86 period and is both lower than the 1.1 per cent recorded between 1974-1980 and considerably less than the 2.8 per cent p.a. average growth of all other manufactured exports in 1980-86. Not only, then, does export volume growth look weak overall but it appears especially so in capital goods.

8.6 The behaviour of capital goods and its implications

The change in the position of capital goods is perhaps especially surprising given the sluggish performance of investment over the last ten years. Although only a full assessment can be made within the context of a well-specified econometric model, it is worthwhile comparing export and import growth of capital goods with their major determinants. Table 8.6 matches the growth of exports of capital goods against the growth of fixed capital formation in OECD countries together with the change in relative unit labour costs; the lower half of the table matches imports with UK domestic fixed capital formation (excluding dwellings), along with the same competitiveness variable.

Table 8.6   *Changes in investment, trade in capital goods and competitiveness (% p.a.)*

Period	UK volume of capital formation[a] goods	Real gross fixed capital	Change in UK competitiveness[b]
		OECD	
Exports			
1970-74	4.6	3.3	-2.9
1974-80	1.1	1.8	7.3
1980-85	1.5	1.7	-2.6
		UK	
Imports			
1970-74	14.3	1.5	-2.9
1974-80	6.0	-0.1	7.3
1980-85	12.6	2.7	-2.6

Notes: [a] Excluding dwellings.
         [b] Negative sign means improvement in competitiveness, and conversely.
Source: MRETS; ETAS; OECD *Historical Statistics*; OECD *Economic Outlook*.

The table illustrates the major difference in demand elasticity between exports and imports. While UK exports of capital goods appear to have kept pace with the growth of OECD investment, UK imports of these commodities have far exceeded the growth of domestic investment with, for example, an annual average growth rate of import volumes of capital goods of over 12.5 per cent in the five years to 1985 compared with a growth in investment of some 2.7 per cent p.a. It is worth noting also that the table suggests an influence of competitiveness, particularly with exports where, for example, growth is higher in 1980-85 than between 1974-80, although OECD capital formation growth was marginally slower and competitiveness had improved. We return to the question of competitiveness below.

The rapid rise in imports of capital equipment has meant a significant increase in the import content of domestic investment. Already by 1979 the average proportion of domestic investment which was supplied from imported manufactured goods had risen to around 19 per cent (derived from CSO, 1983), and the marginal import propensity of investment was higher. Without more recent input-output information it is difficult to be precise about the current proportion; but a rough estimate based on trade and investment data suggests it may have risen considerably in the last few years, to around 29 per cent by 1986.

This development is not without significance, since it implies that policy proposals for increased investment may be much weaker in their domestic output and employment effects than many advocates of this approach probably realise. There is also a further dilemma. The great majority of these imported capital goods are likely to be used for investment which raises efficiency. This follows from the fact that output has not risen as rapidly as these imports have grown. Moreover, CBI survey evidence suggests much of the investment in fixed capital in recent years has been motivated by the requirement of raising efficiency rather than for reasons of capacity expansion.

The very fact that capital goods are being imported at such a rate indicates a weakness of the UK economy in supplying high quality capital equipment, and this warrants attention. Since the imports concerned are capital goods, and not simply consumer goods, there is a policy consideration. In the last resort, consumption goods can be foregone either by the deflationary policies referred to at the beginning of this chapter or by import controls. This may stall the growth of standards of living in the short run, but it need not have any appreciable effects on productive efficiency. If, however, the same options are applied to capital goods where the imported equipment is more efficient than that produced domestically, there is inevitably a negative effect on the growth of productive efficiency. The dilemma facing an economy without a plentiful supply of world-class capital goods producers, therefore, is that its growth performance could become highly constrained unless it has sufficient comparative advantage elsewhere to compensate. With North Sea oil revenue, the UK may have been in such a position; but given its lower value there must now be some concern to find alternative revenues which can pay for the strong and rising demand for imported capital equipment. Unless, that is, the UK itself can turn round its capital goods industry sufficiently quickly to avoid this dilemma altogether.

One of the difficulties of the last decade or so in the capital goods sector has been a weak overall growth of domestic demand coupled with rising foreign competition. This has been particularly intense as the demand for investment goods world-wide has been fairly flat. Whereas some time ago the UK maintained a strong competitive position in a wide range of capital equipment, the number of UK companies holding strong market positions has fallen.

This has been most dramatic in mechanical engineering, a sector where the UK traditionally had a comparative advantage. One problem that has emerged recently has been the rapid increase in demand for electrical engineering products at a time when the UK was in a weaker trading position. On top of these general difficulties, the recession of 1980-81 exerted major competitive pressures on UK capital goods producers. Total UK investment in plant and machinery fell by 8 per cent between 1979 and 1981 - a quite dramatic fall when compared with the 0.3 per cent drop in consumers' expenditure over the same period. A consequence of these severe domestic demand conditions appears to have been an especially large reduction in the capital stocks of those industries which primarily produce capital goods.

Taking the period 1979-86 as a whole, however, domestic demand for plant and machinery has kept pace with consumption, with both rising by 16 per cent in real terms. There has been some recovery in the demand for capital goods from the recession but, as noted earlier, with serious supply weaknesses apparent in the domestic capital goods industries, imports of capital equipment have accelerated faster than imports of consumer goods: in value terms imports of capital and intermediate finished goods rose 25 per cent faster than imports of consumer goods over this period.

8.7 The link between services and manufacturing through investment

The main increase in recent UK plant and machinery investment has not been undertaken in manufacturing (even after allowing for leased equipment which is classified to the service sector) but has been in services, particularly in the distributive trades and financial and business services. It represents one of the strongest links between services and manufacturing since the capital equipment used by the service sectors is largely supplied by the manufacturing sector. In 1979, the latest year for which the relevant information can be deduced, nearly 40 per cent of all investment in plant and machinery was undertaken by service industries (virtually equalling manufacturing investment in these goods) and of this, over three-quarters was supplied by the manufacturing sector, by both home and foreign producers. The net value of the market for manufactured investment goods sold to services in 1979 was over £4bn (equivalent to almost £7.5bn at today's prices), with machinery of a similar value sold by manufacturing industry to itself.

Input-output calculations based on 1979 data show that, of the total purchases by manufacturers of plant and machinery investment goods, 30 per cent were imported - much higher than the 19 per cent quoted earlier in relation to total investment. For purchases by service industries the figure is higher still. In 1979 an average of 33 per cent of investment goods in plant and machinery purchased by services from manufacturing were imported.

A more detailed investigation of purchases by service industries of manufactured investment goods (other than vehicles, etc. and leased equipment), again based on 1979 input-output information, reveals that the principal purchases were telecommunications and other electronic equipment, office machines and computer equipment, various types of mechanical engineering products, office furnishings, and instrument engineering goods. Among these commodities, furniture and mechanical engineering products had the lowest average import propensities, telecommunications equipment about the same as the overall average (*viz.* 33 per cent), while instrument engineering at 42 per cent and office machinery and computer equipment at 77 per cent were the most import-intensive. It is not possible to estimate figures for 1986 but, with the larger part of the domestic demand increase for capital goods coming from service sectors and with some of the major products already highly import-intensive, it is not difficult to conclude that a significant element of the recent rise in imports of capital goods has been destined for service industries. This is, of course, in addition to the increasing use of imported capital equipment within the manufacturing sector. We turn next to a disaggregated picture of these imports of capital goods both by product and by country of origin.

8.8 Trade in capital goods: a disaggregated picture

Table 8.7   *The value of UK imports of capital goods[a]: a commodity breakdown, 1978 and 1985 (£m)*

SITC Code (Rev 2)		1978	1985
71	Power generating machinery and equipment	812	1996
72	Machinery specialised for particular industries	1083	2327
73	Metalworking machinery	320	526
74	General industrial machinery and equipment and parts	1187	2605
75	Office machines and automatic data processing equipment	1105	4512
76(part)	Telecommunications equipment	116	575
77(part)	Electrical machinery and parts	951	3468
782	Motor vehicles for the transport of goods or materials	155	511
87	Professional, scientific and controlling instruments and apparatus	555	1764
81(part), 88(part), 89(part)	Other capital equipment	49	93
Total capital goods		6333	18377

Note: [a] Includes some intermediate goods such as parts of capital equipment.
Source: NEDO, DOTS databank.

Table 8.7 gives a detailed breakdown of UK capital goods imports from the rest of the world between 1978 and 1985. This definition of capital goods is not identical to the one used earlier since it is both expressed in values (rather than volumes) and includes a number of machine parts which were earlier classified under intermediate goods. The overall profile is, however, similar to the one used previously. The table shows that the fastest growth of imported capital equipment was recorded for office machinery and electrical and electronic equipment. Moreover, because of their weight in the total, about 40 per cent of the total growth of capital goods imports during this period can be attributed to computers, telecommunications and other electrical equipment, rising from £2.2bn in 1978 to £8.6bn in 1985.

Most of the absolute increase in imported capital goods has originated from the USA and West Germany, as the weighted contribution column in Table 8.8 shows. Faster growth rates have occurred in Japan and

Table 8.8   *The growth of UK imports of capital goods by country of origin, 1978-85*

Country	Average annual growth of imports	Weighted contribution to average growth (1978 weights)	Value 1985 £m	Per cent
OECD total	14.8	14.0	16837	91.6
of which				
USA	16.3	3.9	4748	25.8
West Germany	12.5	2.9	3511	19.1
Japan	24.3	1.1	1534	8.3
France	10.3	1.1	1397	7.6
Netherlands	15.0	0.9	1117	6.1
Italy	14.1	0.8	977	5.3
Non-OECD total	21.5	1.2	1540	8.4
of which				
Singapore	34.0	0.1	181	1.0
Hong Kong	26.5	0.1	173	0.9
Taiwan	27.8	0.1	145	0.8
World total	15.2	15.2	18377	100.0

Source: NEDO DOTS Databank.

other Far Eastern countries such as Singapore, Hong Kong and Taiwan, but it is only Japan that has substantially increased its market share during the period, from 4.4 per cent to 8.3 per cent.

It has already been noted that the performance of UK exports of capital goods has been somewhat muted in the last decade, particularly in comparison with the growth of imports. Measured in value terms, exports of capital goods on the wider definition used in Tables 8.7 and 8.8 grew by 9.9 per cent p.a. between 1978 and 1985, while imports rose at a rate of 15.2 per cent p.a. It is instructive, however, to consider the performance in trade balance terms as between the sub-categories of goods defined above. Table 8.9 summarises a number of aspects of this. In the first two columns are shown the competitiveness measures as defined earlier for these capital goods categories in 1978 and 1985. This shows that, in 1978, the UK had a strong competitive position in trade balance terms in telecommunications equipment, power-generating and specialised machinery, and trucks. In other areas performance appears adequate in the sense that a balance-of-payments surplus was being

Table 8.9 *Market growth and UK competitiveness in capital goods trade, 1978-85*

SITC Code (Rev 2)	Competitiveness ratio (X-M)/(X+M)		Change	Market growth %	Balance of trade (1978) £m	Share (1978)
	1978	1985				
71 Power generating machinery	0.37	0.21	-0.16	96.5	957	15.9
72 Specialised machinery	0.33	0.14	-0.20	66.2	1086	20.1
73 Metalworking machinery	0.09	-0.01	-0.10	48.3	66	4.4
74 General industrial machinery	0.22	0.06	-0.16	83.1	652	18.7
75 Computer equipment, etc.	-0.09	-0.09	nil	308.1	-186	12.5
76 Telecommunications equipment (part)	0.47	0.03	-0.44	171.3	203	2.7
77 Electrical machinery (part)	0.13	-0.04	-0.17	206.3	276	13.4
782 Trucks, etc.	0.54	-0.15	-0.67	32.5	361	4.1
87 Instruments	0.11	0.10	-0.01	214.5	135	7.7
81, etc. Other capital equipment	-0.21	-0.28	-0.07	79.0	-17	0.1
Total capital goods	0.22	0.04	-0.18	135.4	3533	100.0

Source: Derived from OTS.

generated. However, the exception to this was in office machinery and computer equipment, where the balance of trade was already in deficit. By 1985, the overall competitive position had deteriorated and this was particularly sharp in trucks, telecommunications equipment and some mechanical and electrical engineering areas. The change in competitive position is illustrated in the third column of the table and it can be seen that in no case did it improve. However, one interesting result of this calculation is that the UK's comparative advantage on this basis did not apparently decline in the office machinery and computer equipment area.

In balance-of-trade terms, the story of course does not end with this competitiveness measure. Of great importance is the size of the market, its rate of growth and whether or not there was a deficit at the beginning of the period. The remaining three columns of Table 8.9

complete the picture. There it can be seen that some products, such as trucks, have a relatively low weight in total capital goods imports and therefore do not make a major contribution to the total deterioration. Conversely, the decline in competitive performance in major product areas, for instance in mechanical engineering products, has had a major influence. It was noted above that there has not been an apparent decline in the competitive position of group 75, computer equipment etc. Nonetheless, the fact that this was in deficit in 1978 and that it has grown extremely fast, quadrupling in value terms in these seven years, means that it goes some way in explaining the overall decline in the capital goods balance of trade. In other fast-growing product areas, such as telecommunications equipment and electrical machinery, it is the competitive decline which explains the worsening position. Finally, the one optimistic note which can be pointed to in the table is the rapid growth of trade in professional and scientific instruments, which have maintained their competitive position and improved their balance-of-trade surplus.

Geographically speaking, there has been a distinct difference in performance of UK capital goods exports as between those going to OECD countries and those going to non-OECD ones. UK exports of capital goods to OECD countries grew over twice as fast as similar exports to non-OECD countries during this period, with the fastest-growing markets being in the USA, West Germany and Italy. Exports to Japan, however, grew only one third as fast as imports.

It is noticeable that in 1978 95 per cent of imports of capital goods were drawn from OECD countries, while only some 59 per cent of UK exports were to OECD countries. The slow growth of non-OECD markets since that time has had a significant and detrimental effect on UK exports and has contributed to the trade deterioration. Thus, for example, while exports to the OECD grew at an annual rate of about 12.5 per cent, UK exports to the Middle East and Africa, which in 1978 together constituted over one quarter of the total market for UK exports of these products (split roughly equally), grew by 4.4 per cent p.a. and 2.4 per cent p.a. respectively. To a large extent, this slow growth can be attributed to the state of demand in these markets: in the case of the Middle East because of the effects of dwindling real oil revenues on large-scale investment programmes, and in that of Africa because of similar effects from weak commodity prices and the particular difficulties of trade with South Africa. But there has also been a slight decline in the UK's share of these markets.

Disaggregation of UK trade in capital goods into mechanical and other heavy industrial equipment (SITC codes 71 to 74 inclusive defined above) and other capital goods, mainly computers and other electronic equipment, reveals that these two categories are expanding at quite different speeds, with electronics, etc. growing more than twice as fast as the other group. It turns out that a similar geographical pattern of trade growth applies to both groups on this disaggregation.

In summary, UK trade performance in capital goods appears to have deteriorated sharply for two main reasons. First, a relatively large concentration on exports of mechanical engineering goods, particularly destined for developing countries, suffered from the drawback of a generally weaker growth in world demand for this type of product and from a slowdown in demand for these imports from developing countries from the late 1970s onwards. On top of this the UK's competitive position also weakened. Second, demand for electronic capital goods both at home and abroad has grown very rapidly during the last ten years, particularly computerised equipment often destined for service industries. While in some of these areas UK export growth kept pace with competitors (with the major exception of Japan), this creditable performance has not been sufficient to prevent a large deterioration in the trade balance in these goods, mainly because of a rapid expansion of the market for computers, etc. in which the UK in 1978 already held a weak position and was in trade deficit. Thus, for instance, UK trade in electronic capital goods with the OECD, where UK export growth was not far behind growth in imports, moved from a deficit of £0.4bn in 1978 to a large deficit of £2.2bn in 1985.

8.9 Possible trade-improving influences

From the analysis of this chapter the UK's balance of trade position in the (partial) post-oil era appears to continue to suffer from certain adverse trends. There is evidence that the UK has failed to maintain a competitive position in some areas but, perhaps even more important, has also been unable to increase its market share in a number of rapidly expanding products. Notwithstanding the strengthened invisibles position, these structural imbalances will need to be corrected before long if a return of the balance-of-payments difficulties of earlier years is to be avoided.

In some respects, however, there are elements which may turn out to have important effects in reversing the developments on the non-oil account of the last decade. One of these is the extent of inward direct investment, for example by Japanese companies aiming to export to the rest of Europe from the UK, where there can be an immediate apparent improvement in UK exports and, subject to local content conditions, similar beneficial effects through import substitution. It is possible that in the next decade the consumer goods trade deficit, expressed as a proportion of GDP, will be reduced through this mechanism because of the current import 'saturation' of many consumer products. In the case of capital and other manufactured goods, which on the whole have not yet been completely overtaken by imports, reversal of the adverse trends may be more difficult, although inward investment will have similar beneficial effects on the balance of trade. The recently opened IBM plant at Greenock in Scotland, for example, is already helping to slow the decline in the capital goods trade balance.

Despite the beneficial effects of inward direct investment, it remains small in comparison with domestic investment and there is of course a reverse effect if domestic companies decide to locate a new plant overseas rather than in the UK. In the end much depends on the competitiveness of UK industry. Here, too, there is scope for optimism since one of the consequences of the fall in oil prices has been a parallel depreciation of sterling against most competitor currencies other than the dollar, which has itself been depreciating during the same period. The sterling depreciation of around 25 per cent against the deutschmark since the end of 1985, unlike earlier devaluations, has occurred without a simultaneous impulse to inflation because of the mitigating effects of lower oil prices. Because the government's counter-inflation policy has not been jeopardised this has also meant that corrective action on the part of the authorities has not been required. (For a fuller discussion of this and its implications, see NEDC, 1987.)

While the UK's cost competitiveness has improved substantially against major competitors other than the US (see Fig. 8.8), the likely effects on import and export volumes may not be as strong as desired. Econometric evidence indicates that long-run manufacturing export and import elasticities with respect to cost competitiveness are quite low at about 0.3 and 0.5 respectively (see, for example, UK Treasury, 1986; London Business School, 1986; Bank of England, 1986b). These low elasticities are consistent with the fact that the large deterioration in cost competitiveness between 1978 and 1981 did not apparently change radically the trends in manufacturing exports and imports which, as discussed earlier, were already seriously adverse. Nonetheless, it is possible that the higher volatility of the exchange rate that characterises the whole decade has reduced the estimated elasticities below their 'true' values. Moreover, lags in cost-competitiveness effects may be longer and more indirect than previously supposed, by working through investment decisions.

Be that as it may, the above elasticities, when combined with the trade-weighted depreciation of sterling of about 12.5 per cent, indicate, *ceteris paribus*, a long-run improvement (i.e. over two years or more) in exports of about 4 per cent and a reduction of manufactured import volumes of about 6 per cent. If divided equally between two years this represents an annual gain of £750m in the volume of total manufactured exports, of which about £100m might be the gain to consumer goods, and £150m to capital goods. Manufactured imports might improve by £1250m, with the import volume of consumer goods and capital goods reduced from what they would otherwise have been by £300m and £250m respectively. The size of such changes more than matches the adverse underlying annual trends noted previously and this will be an important factor in stemming the rate of deterioration in the balance of trade. Indeed, if these elasticities are underestimates the beneficial effects of sterling depreciation will be larger.

Taking these effects and applying them to the ratios (X-M)/(X+M) calculated earlier, the consumer goods index would be higher at -0.34 (compared with -0.37 in 1986) and capital goods at -0.05 (compared with -0.07 in 1986). The effect of the competitiveness gain on the basis of these elasticities is thus rather small in relation to the changes over the last ten years. Furthermore, the change in competitiveness is a step change and may be eroded in time by the UK's tendency to have a relatively high inflation rate. This suggests that the adverse trends described in detail earlier will not necessarily be reversed, at least insofar as they have occurred as a result of non-price factors. For a permanent trend improvement, the UK requires continuing gains in relative unit labour costs, a relative shift in productive capacity in traded goods into the UK and/or a progressive improvement in the non-price competitiveness of existing products.

8.10 Concluding remarks

This paper has focused on trends in the UK's balance of trade and on the strengths and weaknesses of the present position. It was argued that a consequence of the reduced value of the oil surplus is to shift a burden of adjustment onto the manufacturing sector, although it is recognised that improvements in any area are beneficial. While financial and other services have grown rapidly and on the whole may be expected to continue to do so, the earnings here are not currently big enough to bear the burden of adjustment if the existing adverse trends in manufacturing trade continue. Nor can the gains in invisible earnings be counted as a dependable alternative to the need for improvement in the manufactures account.

The analysis suggests the adverse competitive trends that have prevailed in manufacturing trade during the last ten years or more may be beginning to stabilise and indeed might improve slightly in some areas, notably consumer goods. There is, however, the problem that even where a relative competitive decline is halted a trade deficit in an expanding market may continue to widen. This has been a difficulty in consumer goods for some years but it has now also emerged as a problem in the capital goods sector, particularly in such fast-growing areas as computer equipment.

The main implication of the paper appears to be that a major improvement in non-price competitiveness in manufacturing industry is required, coupled with a policy which ensures that those services which can be traded are able to do so at a rapid rate. Undoubtedly many different elements are needed to reverse the adverse trends noted here, and the recent improvement in cost competitiveness is a major supportive change. Ultimately, investment in both manufacturing and services is required - in both human capital through training, R&D, and marketing and intelligence, and in productive fixed capital. This chapter has pointed out that a considerable part of the investment in plant and machinery by both manufacturing and service industries, which enhances competitiveness, is supplied by foreign producers. This already poses some policy dilemmas. As a priority, attention needs to be paid to ways in which the competitive position of the UK capital goods sector can be improved. Failure here will otherwise make the dilemma between the pursuit of a highly efficient domestic productive capability and fast and steady increases in the standard of living more acute.

BIBLIOGRAPHY

Akhtar, M.A. (1981) Income and price elasticities of non-oil imports for six industrial countries, *The Manchester School*, Vol. 49, No. 4, December.

Atkinson, J. and Neager, N. (1986) 'Changing the Patterns of Work', NEDO, London.

Bank for International Settlements (1986) *Recent Innovations in International Banking*, Bank for International Settlements, Basle.

Bank of England (1978) Services in the UK Economy, *Bank of England Quarterly Bulletin*, Vol. 18, No. 3, September.

Bank of England (1985a) Off balance sheet risks, *Bank of England Quarterly Bulletin*, Vol. 25, No. 2, June.

Bank of England (1985b) Services in the UK Economy, *Bank of England Quarterly Bulletin*, Vol. 25, No. 3, September.

Bank of England (1986a) Recent innovations in international banking, *Bank of England Quarterly Bulletin*, Vol.26, No. 2, June.

Bank of England (1986b) North sea oil and gas, *Bank of England Quarterly Bulletin*, Vol. 26, No. 4.

Bank of England (1986c) 'Large exposures undertaken by institutions authorised under the Banking Act, 1979', Bank of England, mimeo.

Barker, T.S. (forthcoming) Exports and imports, in Barker, T.S. and A.W.A. Peterson (eds), forthcoming.

Barker, T.S. and Brailovsky, V. (eds) (1981) *Oil or Industry?*, Academic Press, London.

Barker, T.S. and Peterson, A.W.A. (eds) (forthcoming) *The Cambridge Multisectoral Dynamic Model*, Cambridge University Press, Cambridge.

Blackaby, F. (ed.) (1979) *De-industrialisation*, Heinemann, London.

Byatt, I. *et al.* (1982) 'North Sea Oil and Structural Adjustment', Government Economic Service Working Paper No. 54, Treasury Working Paper No. 22, HM Treasury, London.

CBI (various dates) *Industrial Trends Survey*.

Connor, H. and Pearson, R. (1986) 'Information Technology Manpower into the 1990s', Institute of Manpower Studies, London.

Cooke, G. (1986) 'Technology and Employment in the London Clearing Banks', Banking Information Service, London.

Cornwall, J. (1977) *Modern Capitalism: its Growth and Transformation*, Martin Robertson, Oxford.

Daly, A., Hitchens, D.M. and Wagner, K. (1985) Productivity, machinery and skills in a sample of British and German manufacturing plants, *National Institute Economic Review*, No. 111, February.

Driver, C. and Naisbitt, B. (1987) Cyclical variations in service industries' employment in the UK, *Applied Economics*, Vol. 19, No. 4, April.

Gershuny, J.I. (1978) *After Industrial Society*, Macmillan, London.

Gershuny, J.I. (1983) *Social Innovation and the Division of Labour*, Oxford University Press, Oxford.

Gershuny, J.I. (1985) 'The future of service employment', paper presented at the Conferenza Internazionale del 'Progetto Milano, Tecnologia, Professioni e Città', Milan, Italy.

Gershuny, J.I. and Miles, I. (1983) *The New Service Economy*, Frances Pinter, London.

Gleed, R. (1986) 'Modelling Imports of Manufactures', Government Economic Service Working Paper No. 88, HM Treasury, London.

Goldstein, M. and Khan, M.S. (1978) The supply and demand for exports: a simultaneous approach, *Review of Economics and Statistics*, Vol. 60, pp. 275-286.

Hayes Report (1979) 'The newly industrialising countries and the adjustment problem. A report by a working group', Government Econcomic Service Working Paper No. 18, Foreign and Commonwealth Office, London.

Hill, T.P. (1977) On goods and services, *Review of Income and Wealth*, Series 23, No. 4.

Hindle, T. (1986) Corporate Finance: A Survey, *Economist*, 7 June 1986.

Inman, R. (ed.) (1985) *Managing the Service Economy: Prospects and Problems*, Cambridge University Press, Cambridge.

Key, T.S.T. (1986) Services in the UK economy, *Bank of England Quarterly Bulletin*, September.

Kitson, M. and Tarling, R. (1986)'The Service Sector: the Employment Potential in Expanding Activities', Department of Applied Economics University of Cambridge, mimeo.

Landesmann, M. and Snell, A. (1986) 'Implications of a modernisation strategy for the United Kingdom', Cambridge Growth Project Paper, GPP 582, Department of Applied Economics, University of Cambridge.

Lawson, T. (forthcoming) Earnings and incomes policy, in Barker, T.S. and A.W.A. Peterson (eds), *The Cambridge Multisectoral Dynamic Model*, Cambridge University Press, Cambridge.

London Business School (1986) *Quarterly Econometric Model of the UK: Relationships in the Basic Model*, LBS, London.

Manpower Ltd (1986) 'Flexible Manning in Industry and Commerce', Manpower Occasional Survey No. 3.

Mendis, L. and Muellbauer, J. (1984) 'British manufacturing productivity 1955-83', Discussion Paper No. 32, Centre for Economic Policy Research, London.

Momigliano, F. and Siniscalco, D. (1982) The growth of service employment - a reappraisal, *Banca Nazionale del Lavoro Quarterly Review*, No. 142, September.

MSC/NEDO (1984) 'Competence and Competition, Training and Education in the FRG, the USA and Japan', MSC/NEDO, London.

MSC/NEDO (1985) 'A challenge to complacency: changing attitudes to training', MSC/NEDO, London.

NEDC (1987) 'Britain's New Export Opportunities', National Economic Development Council Paper No. (87)7, NEDC, London.

NIESR (1986) *National Institute Economic Review*, No. 116, August.

Petit, P. (1985) *Slow Growth and the Service Economy*, Frances Pinter, London.

Powell, S. and Horton, G. (1985). 'The Economic Effects of Lower Oil Prices', Government Economic Service Working Paper No. 76, HM Treasury, London.

Prais, S. (1986) Some international comparisons of the age of the machine-stock, *Journal of Industrial Economics*, Vol. xxxiv, No. 3, March.

Rajan, A. (1986) *Services - The second industrial revolution?* Institute of Manpower Studies, Butterworths, London.

Rajan, A. and Pearson, R. (eds) (1986) *UK Occupation and Employment Trends to 1990*, Institute of Manpower Studies, Butterworths, London.

Ray, G.F. (1986) Services for Manufacturing, *National Institute Economic Review*, August.

Robertson, J.A.S., Briggs, J. and Goodchild, A. (1982) *Structure and Employment Prospects of the Service Industries*, Research Paper No. 30, Department of Employment, July 1982.

Rothschild, E. (1981) Review article on US service industries, in *New York Review of Books*, 5 February 1981.

Rowthorn, R.E. and Wells, J.R. (forthcoming) *Economic Development and Structural Change: Britain in the World Economy*, Cambridge University Press, Cambridge.

Singh, A. (1977) UK industry and the world economy: a case of de-industrialisation, *Cambridge Journal of Economics*, Vol. 1, No. 2.

Singh, A. (1979) North-Sea oil and the reconstruction of UK industry, in Blackaby, F. (ed.), 1979.

Singleton, J. (1978) The sectoral transformation of the labour force in seven industrial countries 1920-70, *American Journal of Sociology*, vol. 83, No. 5.

Smith, A.D. (1972) 'The Measurement and Interpretation of Services Output Changes', mimeo, NEDO, London.

Smith, A.D., and Hitchens, D.M. (1985) *Productivity in the Distributive Trades*, NIESR Occasional Paper XXXVII, CUP, Cambridge.

Smith, M. (1986) UK manufacturing: output and trade, *Midland Bank Review*, Winter.

UK CSO (1983) *Input-Output Tables for the UK 1979*, HMSO, London.

UK Department of Employment (1971) *British Labour Statistics Historical Abstract* 1886-1968.

UK Department of Employment (1985) *Employment Gazette*, Vol. 93, No. 7, July.

UK House of Lords (1985) *Report from the Select Committee on Overseas Trade*, (Chairman, Baron Aldington), Vol. I Report and Vol. II Oral Evidence, HMSO, London.

UK Treasury (1986) *Macroeconomic Model Technical Manual*, HM Treasury, London.

Wallis, K.F. (ed.) (1985) *Models of the UK Economy: A Second Review by the ESRC Macroeconomic Modelling Bureau*, Oxford University Press, Oxford.

Whiteman, J. (1981) 'The Services Sector - a poor relation?', NEDO, London.

INDEX OF AUTHORS

175

INDEX OF SUBJECTS

For Product Safety Concerns and Information please contact our EU
representative GPSR@taylorandfrancis.com
Taylor & Francis Verlag GmbH, Kaufingerstraße 24, 80331 München, Germany